BE YOUR OWN CONSULTANT

BE YOUR OWN CONSULTANT

188 Ways to Improve Your Business Operation

Irving Burstiner, Ph.D.

A BIRCH LANE PRESS BOOK
Published by Carol Publishing Group

A Birch Lane Press Book
Published by Carol Publishing Group
Birch Lane Press is a registered trademark of Carol Communications, Inc.

Editorial, sales and distribution, rights and permissions inquiries should be addressed to
Carol Publishing Group, 120 Enterprise Avenue, Secaucus, N.J. 07094

In Canada: Canadian Manda Group, One Atlantic Avenue, Suite 105, Toronto,
Ontario M6K 3E7

Carol Publishing Group books may be purchased in bulk at special discounts for sales
promotion, fund-raising, or educational purposes. Special editions can be created to
specifications. For details, contact Special Sales Department, 120 Enterprise Avenue,
Secaucus, N.J. 07094.

Manufactured in the United States of America
10 9 8 7 6 5 4 3 2 1

Library of Congress Cataloging-in-Publication Data

Burstiner, Irving.
    Be your own consultant : 188 ways to improve your business
operation / Irving Burstiner.
        p.   cm.
    ISBN 1-55972-357-2 (hardcover)
    1. Business consultants.   I. Title.
HD69.C6B86   1996
658.4—dc20   95-47107
                                             CIP

To Razel, with love

CONTENTS

PREFACE

I designed this book as an advisory tool for business owners and executives in all branches of industry and commerce. Whatever the type of business you're in, you'll find it a worthwhile reference guide, a hands-on operations manual written in terms that you'll readily understand.

While writing *Be Your Own Consultant,* I held these three objectives firmly in mind:

■ To show you, the reader, how to examine and then fine-tune every major aspect of your current business operation, much as an outside consultant might do, and thereby deter you from squandering some of your hard-to-come-by capital on consulting services.

■ To suggest hundreds of helpful ideas (in addition to the 188 tips) to help you accomplish this feat.

■ To set you squarely on the road to higher sales and greater profits.

1 / HOW TO BE YOUR OWN CONSULTANT

Over the past decade, the business climate has been stormy. Millions of jobs in industry and commerce have vanished. Corporate downsizing continues to alarm the working public. As companies gear up to confront the upcoming challenges of the twenty-first century, they persist in shedding middle managers by the droves. Contraction, rather than expansion, is fast becoming the norm in industry and commerce. Construction of office buildings, shopping centers, and corporate parks is grinding to a near halt. Each year, more than half a million new businesses are launched, while an approximately equal number of firms close their doors.

A surprisingly high percentage of our nation's established businesses are marginal enterprises that yield meager profits year after year. Many just about break even; even minor errors in managerial judgment can nudge these firms into the red. For most of the distributive trades, annual after-tax profits fluctuate between 2 percent and 4 percent of net sales. Nor do profit margins in the manufacturing sector run much higher. Indeed, many companies fare worse.

What *is* going on? And—what can you do to brighten the future of *your* business?

BENEFITS YOU CAN EXPECT FROM ACTING AS YOUR OWN CONSULTANT

The top two challenges that repeatedly confront and confound most business organizations are: (1) how to increase sales, and (2) how to hold down (and preferably, reduce) operating costs. If and when a management is able to resolve both problems in tandem, a concomitant jump in profits is certain.

Any organization that succeeds at carving a niche in the business world will struggle to maintain its position and to grow. These twin drives motivate management to seek greater revenues and higher profits. Yet, most enterprises never attain much more than about two-thirds of their potential. Even the better-managed, highly successful companies can improve their lot whenever they choose to do so. Unfortunately, most organizations lack the proper motivation to review their status during a profitable year. Only during troubled times or when crises loom suddenly is management prompted to seek outside help to investigate its finances, goals, production setup, marketing strategies and tactics, or the organization itself.

When such situations occur, management may find itself asked to pay exorbitant amounts of money for consulting services, perhaps as much as $50,000, or $100,000, or more. Minimum fees for both management and marketing consultants now run from $500 to $1,000 per day. On a weekly basis, that adds up to between $2,500 and $5,000—*for one person.* A consulting firm may recommend assigning two, three, or more of its people to investigate and suggest improvements in just one functional area such as finances, human resources, marketing, production, or sales. A thorough, across-the-board audit may take months to complete and cost several hundreds of thousands of dollars.

This is capital you can put to much better use!

Why not be your own consultant? At modest expense, you can examine every aspect of your business that an outside expert is likely to probe into and effect changes that will put you squarely on the path to higher sales and greater profits.

A SURE-FIRE PROGRAM FOR INCREASING REVENUES AND PROFITS

This program is designed to save you a needless and grandiose outlay of capital. It stresses the value of acting as your own consultant. It offers you many valuable tips for fine-tuning the more significant aspects of your business operation. Upon implementing these suggestions, you will realize: (1) a rapid increase in sales, (2) higher end-of-year profits, and (3) a stronger, more productive organization.

This approach is founded on these three premises:

1. The output of any machine can be enhanced by improving every one of its working parts.

2. Every profit-oriented enterprise *can and should be* viewed as a complex machine designed to produce income for its owner(s).

3. A critical examination of each of the various components of your business (your "money-making machine") should lead to many useful ideas for improving overall performance and increasing total output.

START BY REVIEWING
THE MAJOR PARTS
OF YOUR BUSINESS OPERATION

How much time will you need to spend on the program? Probably at least a week on each of the nine areas. To find the time, delegate a few of your less important responsibilities to others in your organization.

The chart in Figure 1-1 depicts the components of your business to target for examination and improvement. Take one area at a time. For valuable insights into how your operation has been doing, start with the financial end. After you've completed your investigation of this area and have implemented changes for the better, proceed to the operational area where you think you may be able to make the most progress. (Yes, you can skip around; you do NOT have to read the remaining chapters in the order in which they appear! But—you should, sooner or later, explore all remaining segments of your business.)

Here are the nine major areas, along with the more significant subtopics of concern within each area:

- **The financial end.** Financial ratios, cash flow, obtaining capital, asset protection, theft reduction, taxes

- **Human resources.** Organization, staffing, pay plans, training, productivity

- **The business facility.** Location, layout, production, warehousing, physical distribution, systems

- **The product/service mix.** Forecasting, the product line, product development, inventory control, purchasing

- **Pricing.** Pricing objectives, pricing approaches, pricing policies, markup pricing, markdowns and discounts

- **Advertising.** The promotion mix, advertising, message strategy, media selection, promotional techniques

Figure 1-1. Target areas for improvement

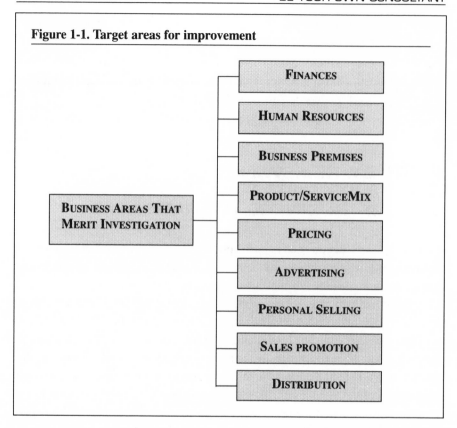

- **Personal selling.** The salesforce, the "80-20" Rule, personal selling, telephone selling, the sales office
- **Promotools.** The promotion calendar, promotion planning, displays, public relations, publicity, differentiating the firm
- **Distribution.** Distribution methods, distribution approaches, product/service delivery, franchising

2/ FINE-TUNE YOUR FIRM'S FINANCES

No aspect of business management is as complex or requires as much attention as the financial area. Money is the lubricant that makes your enterprise run. It pays for the purchase of raw materials and components, goods for resale, installations, supplies, promotion, and distribution. It keeps your employees working at their tasks, pays your rent and other overhead expenses, and gives you some profit. Funds must flow continuously into and out of your operation; without this lubricant, your moneymaking machine will surely grind to a halt.

You can check this for yourself. Get a copy of the *Business Failure Record*, an annual publication of the Dun & Bradstreet Corporation. You'll discover that eight out of every ten companies that fail attribute their demise principally to *economic* and *financial* factors. Most often cited among these reasons for failure are insufficient profits, industry weakness, inadequate sales, heavy operating expenses, burdensome institutional debt, and insufficient capital.*

PROBLEM INDICATORS IN THE FINANCIAL AREA

Here are some troubling symptoms that should trigger your immediate concern:

- Dwindling profits
- Rising expenses
- Having to delay paying your bills
- Having to forego cash discounts offered by suppliers for early payment of invoices

---

*See The Dun & Bradstreet Corporation, *Business Failure Record: 1991 Final/1992 Preliminary* (New York: The Dun & Bradstreet Corporation, 1993), p. 19.

- Accumulating an increasing number of past-due receivables
- Finding it difficult to borrow funds for additional inventory or capital purchases
- Climbing insurance costs
- Stock shortages reaching a worrisome level
- Incidences of pilferage, till-tapping, or other types of internal theft
- Discovering sharp deviations in actuals from your sales, expense, cash, and/or other budgets
- Believing that you have been paying too much in taxes

Figure 2-1 displays target sectors for investigation in the financial management area. These aspects are discussed, one by one, over the balance of this chapter.

KEEP CLOSE TABS ON YOUR BUSINESS OPERATION WITH THESE CRUCIAL FINANCIAL RATIOS

Perhaps the most valuable step you can take to strengthen your operation is to analyze, on a regular basis, certain financial ratios that you can calculate readily from the information in your two basic accounting documents.

> ## —Tip 1—
> **Pull a balance sheet and income statement every quarter, rather than once a year.**

Have your accountant prepare these documents for you every three months. Never allow more than this span of time to slip by before you discover how you have been doing. Any longer than that and it may be too late for you to effect changes for the better. If your operation is sizable or complex, getting your statements each and every month is even more desirable.

Better still, you can save hundreds of dollars annually by computerizing your operation. You'll find it easy enough to do your own bookkeeping on a personal computer (PC). For a modest investment of under $2,500, you can purchase both a user-friendly PC (an IBM, Leading Edge, or Macintosh, for example) and

Figure 2-1. Financial aspects to target for investigation

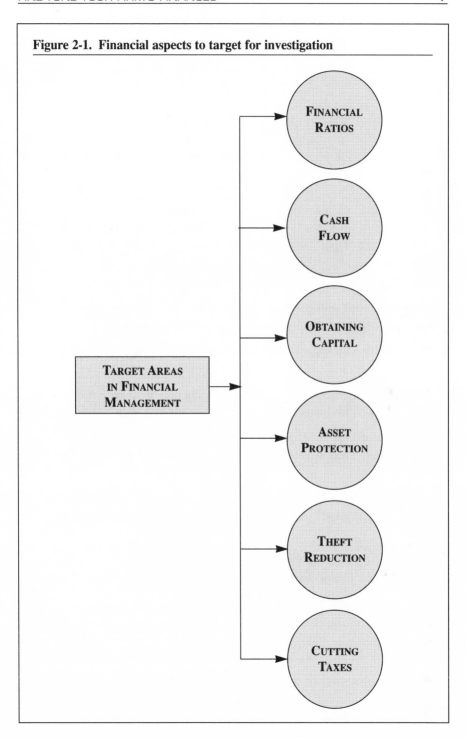

a good printer. Software programs for maintaining ledgers and books of accounts, preparing payrolls and printing checks, and keeping inventory records are readily available; Intuit's QuickBooks and Quicken—and DacEasy Accounting—are examples.

Get Acquainted With Financial Ratio Analysis

By closely monitoring certain key ratios derived from the data on your basic accounting documents, you'll be able to run your operation much better. You'll understand what is—or what has been—going on in your business as you compare each new set of ratios with: (1) your past ratios, and (2) the equivalent ratios of other companies of your type and size. Such comparisons will also enable you to spot important trends early enough for you to decide how best to take advantage of them.

Useful financial ratios fall into three categories:

■ **Liquidity ratios** indicate how solvent your operation is: how easy (or how difficult) it would be for you to pay off your firm's indebtedness

■ **Profitability ratios** show how profitable or unprofitable your operation has been

■ **Activity ratios** reveal the percentage of sales revenues produced in terms of how much you have invested in inventory, total assets, or working capital

Some of the most useful financial ratios are described in figure 2-2. Two of the four liquidity measures shown, the *current* and *quick* ratios, need to be closely watched.

—Tip 2—

Begin the ratio analysis process by calculating both current and quick ratios from the information on your most recent balance sheet.

Let's review the procedure for computing these two liquidity ratios:

1. Copy the appropriate formulas from figure 2-2 onto a sheet of paper.

2. Study the sample balance sheet in figure 2-3, then find and substitute the correct figures for the terms in the formulas.

3. Solve the equations in this fashion:

Figure 2-2. Some significant financial ratios

Liquidity Ratios:

$$\text{Current Ratio} = \frac{\text{Current assets}}{\text{Current liabilities}}$$

$$\text{Quick Ratio} = \frac{\text{Cash} + \text{Negotiable securites} + \text{Accounts receivable}}{\text{Current liabilities}}$$

$$\text{Debt-to-Assets Ratio} = \frac{\text{Total debt}}{\text{Total assets}}$$

$$\text{Debt-to-Net Worth Ratio} = \frac{\text{Total debt}}{\text{Total net worth}}$$

Profitability Ratios:

$$\text{Gross Margin-to-Sales Ratio} = \frac{\text{Gross margin}}{\text{Net sales}}$$

$$\text{Operating Expenses-to-Sales Ratio} = \frac{\text{Operating expenses}}{\text{Net sales}}$$

$$\text{Profit-to-Sales Ratio} = \frac{\text{Net profit (after taxes)}}{\text{Net sales}}$$

$$\text{Cost of Goods-to-Sales Ratio} = \frac{\text{Cost of goods}}{\text{Net sales}}$$

$$\text{Return on Assets} = \frac{\text{Net profit (after taxes)}}{\text{Total assets}}$$

$$\text{Return on Net Worth} = \frac{\text{Net profit (after taxes)}}{\text{Net worth}}$$

Activity Ratios:

$$\text{Rate of Inventory Turnover} = \frac{\text{Net sales}}{\text{Average inventory}}$$

$$\text{Asset Turnover} = \frac{\text{Net sales}}{\text{Total assets}}$$

$$\text{Capital Turnover} = \frac{\text{Net sales}}{\text{Working capital}}$$

Figure 2-3. A sample balance sheet

ASSETS

Current Assets

Cash	$5,760	
Negotiable securities	900	
Accounts receivable, net	10,080	
Inventories	28,035	
Total current assets		$44,775

Fixed Assets

Machinery and equipment, less depreciation	$25,960	
Furniture, less depreciation	13,135	
Delivery truck, less depreciation	15,060	
Total fixed assets		$54,155
Total Assets		$98,930

LIABILITIES AND NET WORTH

Current Liabilities

Accounts payable	$11,290	
Note payable, 1996	6,000	
Accrued payroll taxes	2,670	
Total current liabilities		$19,960

Long-Term Liabilities

Note payable, 1999	$48,000	
Total long-term liabilities		$48,000
Total Liabilities		$67,960
Net Worth		30,970
Total Liabilities and Net Worth		$98,930

$$(A)\ \text{Current Ratio} = \frac{\text{Current assets}}{\text{Current liabilities}} = \frac{\$44,775}{\$19,960} = 2.24$$

(B) Quick Ratio $= \dfrac{\text{Cash} + \text{Negotiable securities} + \text{Accounts receivable}}{\text{Current liabilities}}$

$$= \frac{\$5,760 + \$900 + \$10,080}{\$19,960} = \frac{\$16,740}{\$19,960} = 0.84$$

Read the results as follows: The current ratio is 2.24 to 1; the quick ratio is 0.84 to 1.

Most likely, you're already aware of the rough rule-of-thumb guidelines by which knowledgeable managers judge a company's ability to liquidate its current obligations. A current ratio of 2 to 1 or higher is generally accepted as satisfactory evidence of the firm's financial well-being. So is a quick ratio of *at least* 1 to 1.

While the current ratio in this instance appears satisfactory, the quick ratio points up an incipient problem that may call for immediate action.

Which is exactly why we recommend that you analyze these two ratios in tandem!

The quick, or "acid-test," ratio is a more exacting measure of a company's liquidity than the current ratio. Its formula is basically the same, with this exception: inventories are dropped from the fraction's numerator. Inventories are ignored because they cannot easily be converted into cash with which to pay off current indebtedness.

—Tip 3—

To maintain your firm's financial health, act to bring both current and quick ratios well into line before the end of the next quarter.

Translating the 0.84 to 1 ratio into more understandable terms, this small firm can raise no more than 78 cents in "ready assets" to redeem each dollar of its current liabilities.

Actions to Consider:

Review the two formulas. Obviously, you can improve either ratio by (1) increasing the total amount in the fraction's numerator, and/or (2) reducing the total in its denominator.

To raise the numerator, consider:

- Augmenting your cash balance by ploughing back some of your profit into the business
- Buying additional securities with profit dollars
- Adding more funds to your original investment
- Obtaining cash by selling some shares of stock in your corporation
- Building up your accounts receivable
- Acquiring new equity capital by taking on a partner

    You can lower the denominator by:

- Paying off some current debt with the proceeds from a new, long-term loan*
- Sending in the tax monies you've accrued
- Paying off some of your accounts payable

Profitability Ratios

Of the six measures of profitability shown in figure 2-2, the two that should concern you most are the **gross margin-to-sales** and **operating expenses-to-sales** ratios.

—Tip 4—

**Determine your gross margin-to-sales ratio,
decide whether or not it's satisfactory, and
improve it if you need to.**

An Illustration: You and your partner own a neighborhood hardware store. You have just reviewed your income statement for the first quarter of the year; it presents the following data:

Net sales	$543,040
Cost of goods	360,470
Gross Margin	$182,570

---

*Even though this new obligation won't be counted among your current liabilities, you'll need to be careful that it doesn't appreciably raise either your debt-to-assets or debt-to-net worth ratio! (See figure 2-2.)

You proceed to compute your gross margin-to-sales ratio in the following manner:

$$\text{Gross Margin-to-Sales Ratio} = \frac{\text{Gross margin}}{\text{Net sales}} = \frac{\$182,570}{\$543,040} = 33.6\%$$

Interpreting the above ratio, your firm collected 33.6 cents over and above the cost of goods on each dollar's worth of merchandise you sold.

Checking this figure against the latest report from your trade association, you learn that other hardware stores of approximately the same size as yours averaged 35.5 percent in their gross margin-to-sales ratios. Disappointed with your below-average performance, you and your partner check your records for the preceding quarter. You discover that your earlier gross margin-to-sales ratio was 34.0 percent. Evidently, it has dropped slightly since the last quarter. On checking still earlier P&L's, you learn that this ratio has been falling for quite some time.

You discuss the problem: what steps you can take to bolster the ratio quickly?

Actions to Consider:

As you know, we obtain the gross margin dollar figure for a specified period by subtracting the cost of goods sold from the sales volume taken in during that period. Consequently, you can raise your gross margin-to-sales ratio by: (1) earning more gross margin dollars on the goods you sell while maintaining the same level of sales, (2) increasing sales without affecting the gross margin dollar figure one way or another, or (3) combining both of these approaches.

Adding Gross Margin Dollars: Here are some suggestions to help you earn more gross margin dollars.

- Raise your selling prices on selected items in your line—or, perhaps, across-the-board.*

- Renegotiate with your *major* suppliers. (Try to persuade them to lower their prices by one or more percentage points.)**

- Add to your line other products that can readily carry higher markups.

- Replace suppliers who ask you to pay the freight charges with others who will bill you *F.O.B. destination.*

---

*See chapter 6.

**See the section on "Four Guidelines for Better Buying" in chapter 5.

■ Pay invoices early so as to take advantage of all cash discounts offered.

■ Reevaluate your discount policies with respect to employees, clergy, senior citizens, and other groups to which you may have been granting discounts.

■ Bring an industrial engineer into your plant to establish ideal time standards for production operations.*

Increasing Sales: Ideas for enhancing company revenues are, of course, distributed throughout this book. They also constitute much of the subject matter in chapters 7 through 9. Here are just a few ideas for boosting sales:

■ Introduce, on occasion, one of the more popular promotional pricing techniques.

■ Devise ads that really get results.

■ Choose those ad media most suited to your purposes and needs.

■ Tap brand new markets with direct mail and/or mail order advertising.

■ Explore the merits and drawbacks of telemarketing for your firm.

■ Improve your sales contingent's selling skills.

■ Create more effective displays.

—Tip 5—

Calculate, then review your operating expenses-to-sales ratio and seek to reduce it.

An Illustration: The last quarter's P&L for an electrical supply wholesaler indicated the following data:

Net sales	$3,835,290
Operating expenses	$1,311,950

Here is how the company's controller determined the latest operating expenses-to-sales ratio:

---

*See section on "Four Tips for Refining and Streamlining Operations" in chapter 4.

$$\text{Operating Expenses-to-Sales Ratio} = \frac{\text{Operating expenses}}{\text{Net sales}}$$

$$= \frac{\$1,311,950}{\$3,835,290} = 34.2\%$$

This finding compared unfavorably with the prior quarter's operating expenses-to-sales ratio of 31.1 percent, prompting a personal visit to the bank to consult the latest *Annual Statement Studies*.* The controller was even more dismayed on learning that the operating expenses of other electrical supply distributors averaged only 30.2 percent of sales.

Actions to Consider:

Again, you face three choices when trying to lower your operating expenses-to-sales ratio: (1) cut expenses while still maintaining your customary sales volume, (2) increase sales without modifying your operating expenses in any way, or (3) for the sharpest improvement in the ratio, do both—cut down on expenses and boost your sales volume.

Cutting Expenses: Dig out your income statement from the prior quarter. Place it alongside of your latest P&L. Compare the two statements *line by line* while you mull over the harsh realities of your operating expenses.

What can you cut back on? Obviously, you can't lower your rent or other fixed costs. Concentrate on those costs you can control. Salaries and wages, sales promotion, advertising, inventory, and insurance are promising areas. Reducing your outlays for such classifications as dues and subscriptions, stationery and printing, or travel and entertainment won't yield all that much gain.

You can, of course, take a lower salary for yourself. Or shave $20,000 to $30,000 (or more) off your operating expenses by dropping one full-time employee from the payroll. Or save on benefits by replacing several workers with temps.

Increasing Sales: (Suggestions for boosting sales appear in the earlier section on the gross margin-to-sales ratio.)

---

*Compiled and printed each year by Robert Morris Associates (of Philadelphia), this publication goes out to loan officers at banks across the nation.

Activity Ratios

Of the three activity ratios presented in figure 2-2, one is of singular importance to your decision making: the **rate of inventory turnover**, more popularly known as **stockturn**.

—Tip 6—

Earn more profit dollars by speeding up your rate of inventory turnover.

In the formula for the rate of inventory turnover (figure 2-2), only the denominator needs to be explained. The term **average inventory** represents the average value of inventory maintained and made available for sale during a specified period. Many companies count their goods only once each year; others take physical inventory twice a year; still others do it every quarter or every month. The firm that takes stock annually determines its average inventory by adding the total stock valuations of two separate inventory counts—one at the beginning of the year (B.O.Y. stock) and the other at the end of the year (E.O.Y. stock)—and dividing the sum by two. (*Note:* The E.O.Y. stock for last year becomes the B.O.Y. inventory for this year.)

Thus, a company that takes physical inventory annually relies on two inventory counts, or listings. The two are totaled, and their sum is divided by two to get the average inventory. An organization that takes inventory quarterly will need five listings (the sum of which is then divided by five)—and a firm that takes inventory monthly will require thirteen listings (totaled, then divided by thirteen) to ascertain its average inventory.

An Illustration: Last year, a children's clothing store netted $543,000 in sales. Inventory is taken quarterly. To calculate this retailer's annual stockturn rate, we first need to determine the *average inventory* carried in the store.

Inventory value as of:

January 1	$328,265
April 1	393,910
July 1	401,840
September 1	404,695
December 31	347,770
	$1,876,480 ÷ 5
Average Inventory:	$375,296

Applying the formula, then, we have:

$$\text{Rate of Inventory Turnover} = \frac{\text{Net sales}}{\text{Average inventory}}$$

$$= \frac{\$543,040}{\$375,296} = 1.45X$$

Apparently, then, the average inventory carried by the apparel shop was "turned over" 1.45 times during the year.

—Tip 7—

At least once each year, calculate stockturn rates for different classifications, individual items, and your entire inventory.

Many companies prefer to determine their turnover rates on a quarterly basis. This is even more desirable; doing so becomes a relatively simple matter if your inventory control system is computerized.

Actions to Consider:

You can speed up stock turnover in a number of ways; for example:

- Offer price-sensitive goods on sale at reduced prices.
- Feature displays of the merchandise.
- Show the products in your catalog.
- In the self-service operation, move the items to shelves at eye level.
- Offer early bird or preseason discounts to clear out seasonal inventory.
- Discontinue slow-moving products.
- Replace poor-selling merchandise with items that offer greater sales potential.
- Sell off leftover seasonal goods at sharply lowered prices.
- Beef up your advertising to intermediaries who handle your products.
- Step up the pace of your consumer advertising.
- On occasion, run a special promotional event: a 2-for-1 sale, a premium promotion, a contest, or some other type (see chapter 9).

ADOPT THIS FAIL-SAFE PROGRAM
TO AVOID CASH-FLOW PROBLEMS

Among the most frustrating predicaments that occasionally confront companies of all types and sizes is a negative cash flow—when more money has to be paid out than is coming in. You can, however, readily circumvent unexpectedly running into impediments of this nature by preparing an annual cash-flow budget guide.

—Tip 8—

Forestall cash-flow difficulties with this advance-planning system.

You'll need no more than a few hours of serious planning each year to avoid tight-for-cash situations.

Each year, before September is over, work up a cash-flow chart for the following year. Model it after the one shown in figure 2-4. The chart is based on this simple formula:

Cash (BOM) + Receipts Expected – Disbursements Expected = Total Cash (EOM)

As you may suspect, the initials BOM stand for "Beginning of the Month," and EOM for "End of the Month." Below are brief explanations of the entries you'll need to post in each column:

Cash (BOM): Your estimate of how much company cash should be available on the first day of the month. Include cash on hand, in the bank, and in your petty cash box.

Receipts Expected: Start your calculations by estimating the total sales you think you'll take in during the month. To this figure, add any interest and dividends you're likely to earn on business bank accounts (checking, savings) and company-owned bonds and stocks.

Disbursements Expected: Project the total you'll need during the month to pay all bills, loan installments due, and other obligations.

Total Cash (EOM): To arrive at this figure, add the entries on both lines 1 ("Cash (BOM)" and 2 ("Receipts Expected"). Then, subtract from the resulting sum the amount you've indicated on line 3 ("Disbursements Expected"). This will give you your "Total Cash (EOM)" to enter on line 4.

Figure 2-4. Cash-flow planning chart

	Jan	Feb	March	April	May	June	July	Aug	Sept	Oct	Nov	Dec
Cash, beginning of month												
+ Receipts expected during month												
Total Cash												
− Disbursements expected during month												
Total Cash, End of Month												

When you prepare your chart, start with the January column. Using your best judgment, enter the estimates called for in the appropriate slots. After you have completed all entries for the month of January, transfer the figure on the last line—"Total Cash (EOM)"—to the first line in the February column—"Cash (BOM)." Continue on down the column until you have inserted all estimates required for February. Thereafter, proceed in the same fashion all the way through to the end of the year.

—Tip 9—

Review and adjust your cash-flow chart quarterly.

Your cash-flow chart hasn't been etched in stone. It's not immutable. Four times a year, at the beginning of each quarter, check it over for any adjustments you may have to make to your planned figures. Incorporate those changes into the chart.

—Tip 10—

Determine those periods during the year when your company treasury may become "cash-poor."

As you study the chart, note those periods during the year when your financial situation may become so depressed that you'll want to take immediate steps to improve your cash position. To help you get through the weeks or months that follow, you'll need to tap one or more sources of funds.

Actions to Consider:

Here are some of the steps you can take to improve your company's cash position:

■ Arrange for a bank loan one or two months before the anticipated low-cash period.

■ Make a personal loan to your firm.

- Dispose of excess inventory at once; if you must, sell it out at cost.

- Lease part of your premises to some other business enterprise.

- Cut down on whatever expenses you can; dues and publications, travel and entertainment, and utilities are some of the expense categories to look into.

- Weigh the advantages and disadvantages of replacing your present salesforce with independent sales representatives.

- Sell off unneeded equipment, fixtures, furniture, and supplies.

- Promote an off-price sale.

- Hire one or more temporary employees instead of regular full-time employees.

- Take a cut in salary for six months or more.

- Put off paying your bills for as long as you can.

- Offer higher cash discounts to induce your customers to pay their invoices sooner.

- Factor your accounts receivable.

- Deposit all incoming checks immediately.

—Tip 11—

Tighten internal systems to speed up the collection process.

Bill every customer without delay. Thereafter, carefully monitor all your accounts receivable. If you haven't received payment within a week after the expiration date of the terms you've specified, take immediate action. Photostat the invoice, stamp the copy "PAST DUE" in red ink, and mail it to the customer. Two weeks later, if the account is still open, send the buyer a polite letter suggesting that he or she may have overlooked the bill inadvertently. If this step fails to bring in payment, follow with two or three requests spaced ten days apart. Each letter should convey a stronger tone than the previous one. You might also consider telephoning the account to inquire as to the reason for the excessive delay. If this procedure doesn't work, ask your attorney to contact the customer.

You can avoid many problems of this nature by: (1) investigating and convincing yourself of the buyer's creditworthiness before granting credit, and (2) accepting orders only on a C.O.D. basis from those to whom you've denied credit.

TAP THESE VALUABLE SOURCES OF FUNDS THAT ARE OFTEN OVERLOOKED

At times, you may need a temporary infusion of cash to continue running your operation. Many business owners who find themselves strapped for funds turn to the more customary sources; they'll tap their own savings accounts or certificates of deposit, sell a few securities, borrow from relatives or friends, or seek a bank loan.

There are, of course, other ways of generating working capital.

—Tip 12—

Liquidate assets that are no longer essential to your operation.

Check through all storage areas to find out if there are any machines, equipment, furniture, furnishings, or other company assets that aren't being used and that you may be able to sell. Also look at assets that are currently in use but that you can easily do without.

For a starter, here are some possibilities to look for:

air conditioners	partitions
bookkeeping machines	racks
calculators	refrigeration equipment
carts	scales
cash registers	shelving
coolers	showcases
computers	stands
counters	storage cabinets
duplicating machines	typewriters
heaters	wrapping machines

Sell such items at whatever price you can; you may be pleasantly surprised at the total amount you bring in.

Apply the same thinking to any excess inventory you're holding, company-owned stocks and bonds, cars and trucks, and even buildings.

—Tip 13—

Put up your inventory as collateral for a low-interest loan.

You may be able to obtain a bank loan more readily and at a desirable rate of interest by pledging your finished goods inventory as collateral. In your loan application, show that the market value of your inventory exceeds the amount you request by about one-third.

—Tip 14—

Tap the cash available in your credit card accounts, personal as well as business.

Look over your latest credit card statement(s) to determine how much cash remains available to you under the terms of your credit limit. Draw out the money; pay some of it back monthly, along with the interest due.

If in your estimation you'll have to pay excessive interest charges on balances due, switch to a bank that offers lower rates.

—Tip 15—

Factor your accounts receivable.

Contact a factor who may buy your receivables for perhaps 60 percent to 65 percent of their total value.* This way, you'll get your money up front, instead of having to wait months to collect from all your customers.

—Tip 16—

Borrow the funds you may have accumulated in your life insurance policies.

---

*Factors are companies that are willing to advance money to firms with substantial accounts receivable.

Look over all your life insurance policies except for those that are term life. If you've been paying your premiums regularly for years, you may have built up a considerable amount of cash. Most such policies carry loan privileges; you can borrow some or all of the accumulation at a lower interest rate than you would ordinarily have to pay on a bank loan.

—Tip 17—

Refinance your present mortgage or mortgage other property you own.

If interest rates drop to a substantially more favorable level than you have been paying, look into refinancing the mortgage on your business premises. If this doesn't occur, you might consider extending the length of your present mortgage in order to reduce the amount you're scheduled to pay each month.

You can raise additional capital by securing mortgages on other property you may own, such as vacation home, rental property, a boat, or a private plane.

—Tip 18—

Turn excess space into a cash machine.

Survey your business premises looking for space you aren't using and/or really don't need. If you find some, look for another, noncompeting enterprise whose owners may be willing to rent that space.

—Tip 19—

Arrange for a passbook loan.

Check the current balance(s) in your personal savings account(s). You can use your passbook(s) to obtain an installment loan at an attractive interest rate. As you make your payments, the interest you'll be receiving on your savings will off-set a goodly portion of the charges.

—Tip 20—

Cut your salary!

Although you may be understandingly reluctant to cut back on the remuneration you've been taking out of your business each week, this may be a fruitful avenue for you to follow. Think about this: Reducing your salary by only $100 a week will give you an additional $5,200 a year which you can readily invest in inventory or new equipment!

—Tip 21—

Refinance an outstanding debt.

Discuss with your banker the feasibility of refinancing one or more of your intermediate- or long-term loans.

—Tip 22—

If you've incorporated your business, sell some shares of company stock.

Infuse your treasury with ready cash by selling a modest number of shares of your firm's common stock to employees, relatives, and/or friends. Try to limit the amount of shares you sell to no more than three percent or four percent of company stock.

—Tip 23—

Check into the merits of leasing.

You're facing a dilemma: You need a new piece of machinery, some warehousing or office equipment, a car or truck—but you're short of cash. Don't borrow money to fulfill your need; instead, evaluate the leasing alternative. Leasing will enable you to allocate judiciously the funds that still remain in your treasury.

Incidentally, even labor can be leased. A significant advantage of leasing employees is that you'll save on benefits.

—Tip 24—

Apply for financial assistance from the U.S. Small Business Administration.

If you find yourself short of the funds you need to continue profitable business growth, contact the nearest office of the U.S. Small Business Administration (SBA). Among the SBA's special programs are economic opportunity loans for members of minority groups and disadvantaged persons as well as loans for the handicapped. If these aren't available to you, ask about the procedure to follow in applying for a loan to purchase additional inventory, expand or modernize your plant, or start new construction. (The usual approach is to apply first for a bank loan. If the bank turns you down, you then visit an SBA office to discuss your problem.)

—Tip 25—

Seek venture capital.

Rather than take a new loan, you can seek funding from a venture capital firm or a government-authorized Small Business Investment Company (SBIC). Such organizations are especially willing to invest their capital in young, growing companies in exchange for part ownership of the enterprise.

To apply, you'll need to prepare a proposal that includes, among other pertinent details*:

- A description and history of your firm
- Capitalization
- Financial statements
- Biographical sketches of the owners and key employees
- Principal suppliers

---

*See LaRue Tone Hosmer, "A Venture Capital Primer for Small Business," *Management Aid 235* (Washington, D.C.: U.S. Small Business Administration, 1978), p. 3.

- Sales projections
- Marketing plans

—Tip 26—

Investigate the pros and cons of barter.

If you lack the wherewithal to buy what you need to maintain your business's momentum, consider joining a barter exchange through which you can trade your products and/or services for the goods and/or services of other companies.

EIGHT WAYS TO SLASH YOUR INSURANCE COSTS

Smart risk management can save you many hundreds of dollars annually on insurance premiums. With regard to any type of peril, you may elect to (1) assume the risk yourself, (2) purchase an insurance policy to cover the risk, or (3) transfer the risk to a third party. You can also reduce your chances of suffering a loss by instituting sensible loss prevention measures.

—Tip 27—

Transfer some risk to third parties.

You'll spend less on insurance if you lease, rather than buy, any machinery, equipment, or other forms of property on which the lessors provide insurance. You can also lower your inventory carrying costs by maintaining a lean stock and purchasing small quantities of additional goods only as they are needed. Even further savings may be effected by buying from suppliers who carry product liability insurance.

—Tip 28—

Plan and institute an effective fire-prevention program.

Although the likelihood of suffering a fire on your premises is very low, this is the most serious peril a business can face. A small fire can shut down your operation for days or even weeks; a major blaze can destroy your enterprise totally.

Actions to Consider:

■ If not already required by law, ban smoking throughout your building.

■ Institute a monthly inspection program for scrutinizing every nook and cranny of your business premises: building and grounds; entrances, exits, hallways, doors, elevators, and stairwells; electrical, heating, and air-conditioning/cooling systems; and all fire prevention and firefighting equipment (smoke detectors, fire extinguishers, hoses, sprinkler system, and so on).

■ Charge one person with diligently carrying out this monthly inspection routine (a senior executive, the plant superintendent, or the head of the maintenance department).

■ Advise all personnel of the company's safety rules and programs.

■ Inform all employees as to the locations of firefighting equipment and teach them how to use it.

■ Identify all fire exits with proper signs.

■ Teach your employees how to respond to a fire alarm and conduct fire drills several times each year.

■ Practice good housekeeping: dispose of trash regularly and store chemicals and flammable materials in safe areas and in proper containers.

—Tip 29—

**Implement safety measures to forestall accidental injury
and avoid costly litigation.**

Accidents can happen not only to employees but to shoppers, customers, visitors, sales representatives, or anyone else on or near your premises. Such mishaps can cost you dearly if negligence on your part can be proven. Malfunctioning machinery and equipment aren't the only culprits; an accident can occur just as easily in a hallway, stairwell, office, washroom, lunchroom or cafeteria, mailroom, warehouse, shipping or receiving department, or on the loading dock.

Actions to Consider:

■ Install safety railings around machinery and make certain that all equipment is in good operating condition.

■ Replace worn floor tiles, carpeting, or mats immediately.

■ Insist that your workers wear protective clothing whenever the job requires it.

■ Institute procedures for handling and reporting injuries.

■ Keep walks, entrances, stairwells, floors, and aisles clean, dry, and free of obstructions.

■ Mop up spills and wet floors at once.

■ In rainy weather, lay down rain mats where needed.

—Tip 30—

**Each year, review your entire insurance program
with an experienced professional.**

Situations do change. As an example, property values may go up or down. Enlist the services of an insurance professional who has had considerable experience with your type of business. Meet with that person once each year. Before the two of you get together, though, read through all your policies, paying close attention to the fine print. Go to each meeting prepared to ask questions about anything and everything you don't understand. Discuss your current program and seek advice about the kinds of insurance coverages you may or may not need. Then, devise a modified program for the following year that precisely suits your situation.

—Tip 31—

Stop paying premiums for nonessential insurance.

Cover only those perils you can afford to pay for. Be prepared to absorb small losses that won't appreciably affect your operation. Do you really need protection against glass breakage or water damage? Is business interruption insurance right for you?

If you've been carrying separate power plant or crime insurance, drop those policies and tack both coverages onto your multiperil policy. An endorsement to your fire policy will cover leakage from your sprinkler system.

Here's another money saver: Subscribe to a group health plan to which your employees are also required to contribute.

—Tip 32—

Request higher deductibles and save hundreds of dollars each and every year.

Don't give away money needlessly! By increasing your deductibles on some policies, you may be able to shave your premiums by as much as 20 percent or 30 percent.

—Tip 33—

Never undervalue your business premises to reduce your fire insurance premium.

Avoid the misguided temptation to declare a lower value on your property in order to cut your fire insurance premium. Should you suffer fire damage subsequently, your policy's "coinsurance clause" can cost you dearly. You'll discover, unhappily, that any settlement you receive will be directly proportionate to the percentage by which you undervalued your premises.

—Tip 34—

Record, in detail, all insurance activity.

Maintain accurate, year-round records of all insurance activity, preferably on computer disks. For each policy in effect, set up a separate file and enter such details as:

- Type of policy
- Policy number and date of issue

- Coverage details

- Renewal date

- Name, address, and telephone number of the insurer

- Name, address, and telephone number of your insurance representative

- Notification procedure to follow if a loss is sustained

- Date and description of the loss

- Proof of loss

- How the claim was settled

To provide proof for future claims, photograph or videotape your building; all machinery, equipment, and tools; furniture and furnishings; inventories; and the contents of all desks, bins, closets, and shelves. Store these visual records safely in some location other than on your business premises—and be sure to update them annually.

TESTED TIPS FOR MINIMIZING LOSSES FROM INTERNAL AND EXTERNAL THEFT

Unfortunately, today's business organizations must operate in an environment fraught with perils such as burglary, robbery, pilferage, and other types of crime. Retail enterprises face additional problems; shoplifting, counterfeit money, and bad checks are examples.

Internal Theft

For the vast majority of business organizations, losses due to internal theft exceed by far those from external theft. Topping the list of criminal acts committed by company employees are stealing goods and pilfering money.

An astute management will devise and institute sound procedures to curtail employee theft.

—Tip 35—

Start erecting your antitheft defenses at the very beginning.

One of the best defenses against employee theft is preemployment screening. Before hiring anyone, carefully check that person's references and all other information submitted on the candidate's employment application. Perform a credit check, too.

Another positive move is to enlist the support of your management and supervisory team in establishing an atmosphere within your organization that fosters honesty and good conduct.

—Tip 36—

Refine your procedures for handling cash and checks.

Set up effective internal controls for processing both cash and checks. Take the time, too, to instruct your employees in safe money-handling procedures.

Actions to Consider:

- Cover your employees with a blanket fidelity bond (available from a bonding or insurance company) to protect you against dishonesty by employees with access to large sums of money.

- Keep as little cash on hand as possible.

- Throughout the day, remove $20, $50, and $100 bills from the cash registers as they accumulate.

- Keep the checks and excess cash, along with any rolls of coins you need for making change, in a strong, fire-resistant safe that is bolted to the building.

- Hire a shopping service to test cashiers whom you suspect of till-tapping.

- Incoming mail may contain cash, checks, or money orders. Open the mail yourself or delegate this responsibility to a trusted employee.

- Insist that every customer gets a receipt.

- Forbid employees to pay out cash without your approval.

- Require your approval on all discounts granted to customers or employees.

- Prepare all deposits yourself. If you cannot, designate one employee to take over this chore.

- Personally reconcile every bank statement; examine the cancelled checks that accompany it; and review the endorsements on the checks.

- Try to sign every check yourself; authorize another executive to sign checks whenever you won't be available.

- Carefully examine each invoice before issuing a check for payment.

- Keep the checkbook under lock and key.

- Teach your cashiers how to recognize counterfeit currency. (Note: You might also consider putting in a currency scanner or buying those special pens that can readily identify bills as good or counterfeit by the color that shows up upon marking the bill with the pen.)

—Tip 37—

Take steps to minimize opportunities for an embezzler.

While not all that common, embezzlement by an employee can seriously hurt your operation. To avoid being victimized, establish financial controls that would make it difficult for anyone to juggle your books, kite checks, or engage in lapping (covering shortages by not depositing cash receipts promptly). Here are some of the steps you can take:

- Check your basic accounting statements regularly.

- Monitor your receivables.

- Verify every invoice before issuing a check.

- Require two signatures on every purchase order.

- Bond your employees.

—Tip 38—

Step up internal security to discourage employee theft.

Protect your assets. Place a safety net over your premises and its contents to reduce thefts of merchandise, equipment, supplies, and services.

Actions to Consider:

- Have all employees use the same exit when leaving the premises and station a security guard at that exit.

- Fence off the receiving and shipping areas and place them off limits to unauthorized persons.

- Have the receiving department maintain a daily record in which to log the details of each delivery: the date and time of arrival, shipper's name and address, identity of transportation company, number of cases received and their contents, and so on.

- Keep truck bays under surveillance whenever trucks are loading or unloading.

- Always remain alert for possible collusion in the shipping and receiving departments and in the warehouse itself. Hire a private detective to work, undercover, in the department or area where you suspect stealing may be going on.

—Tip 39—

Cut down on the personal use of company phones, office copiers, and postage.

You may be losing many hundreds, if not thousands, of dollars each year because employees use your telephones, copying machines, and even postage for personal reasons. Cut down immediately on these forms of petty thievery. You can, for example:

- Clearly spell out your policy regarding the personal use of company telephones in your Employees' Handbook.

- Block 900-number calls.

- Review all telephone bills when they arrive and follow up on the source of each long-distance call.

- Whenever possible, fax documents destined for distant cities after 5 P.M. when telephone rates are lower.

- Post notices on all copying machines to the effect that they are "NOT FOR PERSONAL USE."

- Permit only authorized personnel to use postage meters and keep them locked up when not in use.

—Tip 40—

Enact measures to block computer crime.

Safeguard business secrets, along with your files, hardware, and software, by locking up all your equipment and cabinets at the end of each day. Limit access to your computers to only those employees whose work requires it. Be sure to back up all files and change passwords regularly.

External Theft

Among the crimes most often perpetrated against businesses are: attempting to pass bad checks or counterfeit money; use of stolen credit cards; burglary; robbery; and shoplifting.

—Tip 41—

Institute a strict check-acceptance procedure.

To avoid getting stung with bad checks, set up a strict check-acceptance system. Insufficient funds in the customer's checking account isn't the only problem that may crop up. You may be offered checks drawn on accounts or banks that do not exist or checks on which the amounts have been altered. Other problems are legion: checks that carry old dates or are postdated, checks with illegible signatures or evident erasures, second-party checks, and so on.

Actions to Consider:

- Before accepting a check, request two forms of identification: a driver's license (preferably bearing a photograph), car registration, major credit card, or passport are the most suitable forms.
- Refuse checks that bear erasures or are illegible, postdated, or more than thirty days old.
- Checks should be made out for the exact amount of the purchase.
- Accept only checks imprinted with the customer's name and address.
- Never take second-party checks.

—Tip 42—

Fight credit card fraud.

Do not honor any charge card beyond its expiration date or if the signature on the charge slip differs markedly from that on the charge card. If you entertain any suspicions whatsoever, ask to see the shopper's driver's license, compare the signature on it with the one on the charge card, and jot down the license details on the sales slip.

—Tip 43—

Burglar-proof your business premises.

There are measures you can take that will discourage individuals intent on burglarizing your premises from gaining unlawful entry.

Actions to Consider:

- Have a locksmith inspect all doors, door frames, and locks throughout your premises to ascertain whether or not the locks are secure and that doors and frames can stand up to attempts at forced entry.
- Use pin-tumbler type locks that contain five or more pins.
- Install outdoor lighting to illuminate your building at night.
- Post a security guard.
- Install timers on both interior and exterior lights.
- Hire a night security guard.
- Consult a security firm about state-of-the-art equipment such as motion, vibration, and ultrasonic sound detectors and electronic sensors.
- Have the security company survey your premises and install a silent central-alarm system.
- Use windows made of burglar-resistant glass.
- Install bars or gratings over windows and skylights.
- Secure back or side doors with deadbolt locks.
- Keep all keys locked up when not in use. Tag each key with a code letter or number to conceal the identity of the lock it fits.
- Issue as few keys as necessary and keep records of who has which keys.
- Replace a lock immediately if the key has been lost or stolen.
- Bolt your safe to the floor.

—Tip 44—

Implement measures to deter would-be robbers.

With some forethought and careful planning, you can sharply curtail the threat of robbery on your premises. Here are a few useful suggestions for accomplishing this purpose:

- Pay your employees by check, not in cash.

- Keep as little cash as possible on the premises.

- Use an armored car service to transport large sums of money.

- Call the police if you spot suspicious characters loitering on or around your premises.

- Before locking up, check the premises carefully.

—Tip 45—

Take steps to reduce shoplifting losses.

Shoplifting is the number one crime problem for retailers. It is also a most vexing—and most difficult—problem to eradicate. Financial losses from this crime run as high as 5 percent to 6 percent of sales for the majority of retail firms.

Actions to Consider:

- Train employees to be especially wary of lingerers, small groups who enter at the same time, and shoppers carrying large bags or wearing bulky coats.

- Post signs to the effect that packages carried in by shoppers must be left at the desk or with the cashier.

- Put up convex mirrors so that all areas in the store are visible.

- Install closed-circuit TV cameras.

- Provide supervision for dressing rooms.

- Tie down goods on display.

- Equip locked rear doors with alarms.

- Keep close watch on departments where high shrinkage has been reported.

- Attach electronic sensors to garments.

- Employ a plainclothes detective to patrol the store.

- Discourage the switching of price tickets or labels by attaching price tags with strong plastic string, concealing additional price labels inside the package or merchandise, or using tickets that bear identifying punch-hole designs.

- Put up antishoplifting warning signs around the store.

- When shoplifters are caught, PROSECUTE!

FOUR WAYS TO REDUCE YOUR INCOME TAX

You've worked long and hard to build your business. You understand quite well that you'll have to pay income tax but you would like to retain more of your earnings each year. The pressure to hold down your tax liabilities is even greater if you're the sole proprietor—the Self-Employment Tax will kick in and cost you even more.

In addition to taking all the usual business deductions you're entitled to, be sure to explore the following tax-savings.

—Tip 46—

**Take advantage of Uncle Sam's largesse:
Put in for a Section 179 deduction.**

You can deduct up to $17,500 in business expenses for qualifying property you purchase and place in service during the year. Bear in mind, though, that you cannot claim more than the taxable income you derive from your business operation. If your taxable income falls below the $17,500 limit, carry over the difference to next year's tax return.

You don't have to claim the entire amount for the year; if you prefer, you can write off some portion of the deduction and then take depreciation on the balance.

Use IRS Form 4562 to make the election to take this "Section 179" deduction.

—Tip 47—

Tax-shelter part of your income with a qualified retirement plan.

Reduce your federal and state (and, in some areas, local) income tax liabilities by setting up a qualified retirement plan for you and your employees. Contributions to the plan may be made by you or by both you and your employees. These contributions are generally deductible.

There are two types of qualified retirement plans: defined contribution and defined benefits plans. Adopting an existing IRS-approved master or prototype retirement plan is simpler than establishing your own plan.

Defined Contribution Plans: Included in this category are profit-sharing, stock bonus, and money purchase plans. The profit-sharing plan lets your employees or their beneficiaries share in the enterprise's profits. The stock bonus plan works much the same way except that benefits are payable in the form of company stock. The money purchase pension plan is not based on profits; instead, you contribute each year a stated amount or a stated formula (for example, 10 percent of each participating employee's compensation).

Defined Benefit Plans: You'll need professional help to set up a defined benefit plan. Contributions to plans of this type are based on actuarial assumptions.

Retirement Plans for the Self-Employed

Keogh plans may be set up by a sole proprietor or a partnership, but not by a partner. Contributions to the plan are not taxed to employees until plan benefits are distributed to them.

Defined contributions plans: Annual contributions to a profit-sharing Keogh are limited to the lesser of $30,000 or 15 percent of the employee's taxable compensation. (*Note*: With the money-purchase Keogh plan, the percentage jumps to 25 percent.) For plan years beginning in 1994 the maximum compensation that can be taken into consideration is $150,000.

For sole proprietors, the profit-sharing Keogh is based on net earnings and limited to the smaller of $30,000 or 13.0435 percent of net earnings (15 percent reduced). The limit on a money-purchase Keogh plan is the smaller of $30,000 or 20 percent of net earnings (25 percent reduced).

Simplified Employee Pension (SEP) Plans

Less complex SEP-IRA's can be set up for each qualifying employee. Each year, you can contribute up to the smaller of $30,000 or 15 percent of the employee's compensation. If you're a sole proprietor, you're limited to the smaller of $30,000 or 13.0435 percent of your net earnings.

SEP-IRA participants can also contribute up to $2,000 to the plan independent of your contribution. Additionally, a salary reduction (elective deferral) arrangement can also be made.*

—Tip 48—

Earn a substantial tax break by donating slow-selling or out-of-season goods to charities.

A corporation can deduct charitable contributions on its income tax return. Partners or shareholders in a corporation may be able to do the same on their individual income tax returns.

When using the deduction, give the fair market value of the property as of the date it was contributed LESS any gain you would have realized if you had sold the property at its fair market value.**

—Tip 49—

Deduct casualty or theft losses.

You may deduct losses due to theft in the tax year they are discovered. Generally, a casualty loss is deductible only in the tax year in which it occurs. If, however, you suffered the loss in an area that the President of the United States has declared to be eligible for federal disaster assistance, you can choose to declare the loss on your income tax return (or amended return) for the immediately preceding tax year.

---

*For further information, see IRS Publication 560—"Retirement Plans for the Self-Employed" and IRS Publication 590—"Individual Retirement Arrangements (IRAs)."

**See IRS Publication 526—"Charitable Contributions."

Examples of casualty losses are: damage, destruction, or loss due to earthquake, hurricane, tornado, flood, storm, or vandalism; fire damage; and losses resulting from accidents that involve cars or trucks provided that negligence isn't involved or that the accident is a result of a willful act.

To claim a casualty loss, you'll need to furnish full details and show proof of loss. Any insurance monies reimbursed must be subtracted from the amount you claim.

USEFUL REFERENCES

Bintliff, Russell. *Crimeproofing Your Business*, New York: McGraw-Hill, 1994.

Blum, Laurie. *Free Money for Small Businesses and Entrepreneurs*. New York: Wiley, 1992.

Curtis, Bob. *Retail Security: Controlling Loss for Profit*. Stoneham, Mass.: Butterworth, 1983.

Donnahoe, Alan S. *What Every Manager Should Know About Financial Analysis*. New York: Simon & Schuster, 1990.

Farrell, Kathleen L. and John A. Ferrara. *Shoplifting: The Antishoplifting Guidebook*. New York: Praeger, 1985.

Fleury, Robert E. *The Small Business Survival Guide: How to Manage Your Cash, Profits, and Taxes*. Naperville, Ill.: Sourcebooks, 1992.

Gaston, Robert J. *Finding Private Venture Capital for Your Firm: A Complete Guide*. New York: Wiley, 1989.

Glau, Gregory R. *The Small Business Financial Planner*. New York: Wiley, 1989.

Greene, Mark R. and James S. Trieschmann. *Risk and Insurance*, 7th ed. Cincinnati: South-Western, 1988.

Hayes, Rick Stephan. *Business Loans: A Guide to Money Sources and How to Approach Them*, rev. ed. New York: Wiley, 1989.

Milling, Bryan E. *Cash Flow Problem Solver*, 2d ed. Radnor, Pa.: Chilton, 1984.

Neveu, Raymond P. *Fundamentals of Managerial Finance*, 3d ed. Cincinnati: South-Western, 1988.

O'Hara, Patrick D. *SBA Loans: A Step-by-Step Guide*, 2d ed. New York: Wiley, 1994.

Perline, Neil. *The Small Business Guide to Computers and Office Automation*. Chicago: Dearborn, 1990.

Rachlin, Robert. *Total Business Budgeting: A Step-by-Step Guide with Forms*. New York: Wiley, 1991.

Scott, Gina Graham. *Positive Cash Flow: Complete Credit and Collections for the Small Business*. Holbrook, Mass.: Bob Evans, 1990.

Siegel, Joel E., Jae K. Shim, and David Minars. *The Financial Trouble-Shooter: Spotting and Solving Financial Problems in Your Company.* New York: McGraw-Hill, 1993.

Simini, Joseph P. *Budgeting Basics for Nonfinancial Managers.* New York: Wiley, 1989.

The Ernst & Young Tax Saving Strategies Guide, 1994. New York: Wiley, 1994.

Williams, C. Arthur, Jr. and Richard M. Heins. *Risk Management and Insurance*, 6th ed. New York: McGraw-Hill, 1988.

3/ STIMULATE AND INVIGORATE YOUR HUMAN RESOURCES

As we have seen in chapter 2, money is the lubricant that courses through the business enterprise and enables its smooth functioning. Yes, your financial resources are indeed essential, but your human resources are no less essential! They are the people who help you run your moneymaking machine and without whose dedicated effort your business will grind to a halt.

Once you have secured a foothold in our economy, your new company will begin to grow. Its growth may be slow or rapid, perhaps even explosive. As this growth continues, layers of supervision may be added, responsibilities may overlap and blur, more management positions may be created, and job descriptions may change.

PROBLEM INDICATORS IN THE HUMAN RESOURCES AREA

Be prepared to act promptly if any of the following phrases apply to your business operation:

- Rising labor costs
- Confusion over who reports to whom
- Duplication of effort
- Poor interdeparmental coordination
- A worrisome rate of labor turnover
- Difficulty in filling job openings
- Evidence of inadequate training among employees
- Employee-supervisor conflicts

- Signs of deteriorating morale (a high rate of absenteeism and/or tardiness, disgruntled employees, an unusual number of grievances filed, and so on)
- Little or no employee participation in goal-setting or decision-making
- Declining productivity
- Lack of employee enthusiasm for change

To tone up your human resources, you'll need to probe diligently into such trouble spots as those disclosed in figure 3-1.

HOW TO BUILD A MORE EFFECTIVE ORGANIZATION

As a business enterprise meets with initial success and its sales increase, more employees may be needed. Ideally, your organization should be able to handle all the work required to attain the company's goals and yet be a lean, tight structure.

Develop a productive, though lean organization by devoting time and effort to working on and with your human resources.

—Tip 50—

Conduct an audit of your present organization.

While most often applied to finances, audits of other major facets of an enterprise are beneficial and should be conducted every few years. The audit procedure involves: (1) scrutinizing all aspects of an existing situation, (2) seeking and uncovering problem areas, and (3) devising strategies and tactics to resolve all problems and improve the overall situation.

Initiate an audit of your organization by listing on a sheet of paper the names and job titles of all your present employees. From this information, prepare an organizational chart; it will serve you as a tool for digging more deeply into the human resources area.

—Tip 51—

Rationalize your organizational chart with the basics of organization theory.

Figure 3-1. Human resources aspects to target for investigation

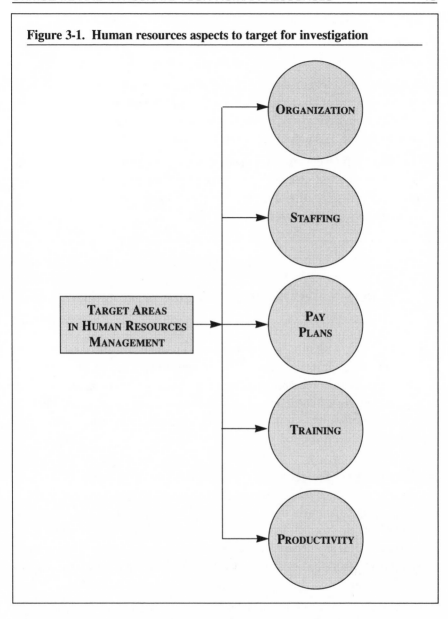

Check for possible flaws in your organizational structure. See if your chart conforms to the principles of organization theory indicated below:

■ **Specialization of Work.** All activities that must be performed so that your company can fulfill its mission and attain its objectives have been assigned to specific and discrete functional areas within the organization.

- **Unity of Command.** No employee reports to more than one superior.

- **Span of Authority.** No department or section head, supervisor, or other manager has too many subordinates reporting to him or her.

- **Flat, Not Tall Organization.** Several layers of management haven't been interposed between the top executive team and the rank and file. (Too hierarchical a set-up slows down internal communications, renders the organization more inflexible, and reduces company output.)

- **Line and Staff Organization.** Responsibilities have been assigned and appropriate authority delegated to all those along the chain of command. Employees in advisory, technical, and other specialized capacities are entrusted with authority only over their own areas and staffs.

—Tip 52—

Review every department in your organization.

One by one, scrutinize every department in your company to determine how each fits into and contributes toward the entire operation in accord with your company's rationale, mission, and long-term objectives. Probe all aspects of each department: its basic function (and the function of each section), the kinds of work being performed, positions, methods, systems, relationships with other departments and sections, and so on.

Actions to Take:

- Justify every department in your company. Does the work of any department encroach in any way on the domain of another department? Is effort being duplicated? Has any department outlived its usefulness? Can you reassign one department's workload to another department? Can you combine two departments into one?

- Within each department, review all sections. Is every section necessary to the operation? Can one be dropped and its work activities be transferred to another section? Is there evidence of duplication of effort? Would it be advantageous to combine two sections into one?

- Analyze positions in each department. Are they all needed? Can one be dropped and the responsibilities shifted to someone else in the department? Has anyone been performing work that lies well outside of his or her assigned responsibilities? Do all positions require full-time workers or can one or more be filled with part-timers?

—Tip 53—

Draft updated job descriptions for all current positions.

From the job analyses you've just conducted, prepare written job descriptions to keep on file. Each sheet should show the job title, duties, responsibilities, work conditions, organizational relationships, and other useful information. You can use these sheets in the future to develop job specifications for each position; these "specs" will describe the skills, work experience, level of education, and other qualifications desired in job applicants for those positions.

—Tip 54—

Evaluate all current personnel in light of the new job descriptions.

Referring in each case to the appropriate job description, assess the value of all current personnel. Complete for each employee a form that contains the following information:

- Name of employee
- Title of position
- Employee's major strengths
- Employee's major weaknesses
- An estimate of the employee's growth potential

File the information in the employee's folder; you'll refer to the form when planning for organizational development and growth.

—Tip 55—

Project likely organizational growth for the next five years.

As you begin planning for your firm's future, you'll want assurance that you'll have the right people in the right jobs at the right times. You'll get that assurance by designing an effective long-range program for the acquisition, training, and development of your company's human resources. To formulate a program of this nature, you'll need information on such external and internal factors as:

- The state of the economy—now and over the next few years
- Population trends
- Technological change
- Social changes
- Changes in the industry
- Political and legal influences
- Competitors' strategies and tactics
- Estimated employee turnover rate
- Projected increases in promotion budgets
- Plans for expansion, contraction, or diversification
- The scheduled introduction of new machinery and/or equipment
- The opening of new markets

Actions to Consider:

- Project, year by year, your personnel requirements for the next five years.
- Review your list of current personnel and decide to which job on your "future needs" list each employee will be assigned.
- Determine how many more people you'll need to hire and the kinds of positions they'll be filling.
- Set up a timetable to accomplish this organizational growth. Bear in mind that much time will be needed to locate, interview, hire, and train people for the additional positions.

MEASURES YOU CAN TAKE TO IMPROVE YOUR STAFFING PROCEDURES

All throughout your investigation into the staffing process, be sure to adhere strictly to the antidiscrimination guidelines of the following federal laws (and their subsequent amendments):

- The Equal Pay Act (1963)
- The Civil Rights Act (1964)
- The Age Discrimination in Employment Act (1967)
- The Equal Employment Opportunity Act (1972)
- The Americans with Disabilities Act (1991)

  Staffing activities include:

- Locating and developing labor sources
- Recruiting
- Screening job applicants—interviewing, testing, reference checking, and perhaps conducting medical examinations
- New-hire orientation, probation, and evaluation

—Tip 56—

Postpone hiring an additional employee as long as you can.

As sales continue to rise, management may be tempted to add one or more employees to assist with the increasing workload. The thought is not unattractive, of course; hiring someone to take over some lower-level chores would free the owner or manager for more important activities.

Be careful, though; don't add to your payroll until you absolutely must! There's sound reasoning behind this caution: You would need a sizable increase in sales just to offset the cost of another employee.

To demonstrate this fact, assume that your income statement for last year shows the following statistics.

Category	Dollar Amount	Percent of Total Sales
Net sales	$500,000	100%
Cost of goods	265,000	53
Gross margin	$235,000	47%
Operating expenses	195,000	39
Profit (before taxes)	$40,000	8%

Now, let's suppose that you had hired a new employee at the beginning of last year at a modest annual salary of $20,000. As you no doubt would have discovered, you were compelled to add about one-third more to that salary to cover both the fringe benefits you paid for and the employer's contribution to Social Security taxes. Your actual expenditure for the new worker came to $27,000.

Look at the income statement again. If your net sales, cost of goods, and all operating expenses—other than payroll—had remained the same, your bottom-line figure would have dropped from $40,000 to $13,000. The $27,000 spent for the new employee would have been subtracted directly from your before-tax profit. Percentagewise, that profit would have dropped from 8 percent of sales to 2.6 percent. That's a 67.5 percent decline!

To have ended up the year with the original amount of profit ($40,000), you would have needed an additional $57,447 in sales—or more than double the amount that you laid out for the new worker!

—Tip 57—

Refine and strengthen your recruitment and selection procedures.

How do you find new employees? Do you depend for the most part, as many companies do, on jobseekers who stop by your place of business? Or on resumés that arrive in the mail? Or on recommendations from employees, friends, relatives, or neighbors? Or on signs you put up on your window or notices you post on your bulletin board?

Be aggressive in your recruiting efforts! Cultivate and pursue other recruitment approaches as well; for example:

■ **For most part-time openings:** Contact academic and commercial high schools, trade schools, and colleges in your area; temporary help agencies; public employment agencies

■ **For many entry-level, full-time positions:** Approach the above-mentioned educational institutions; place classified ads in the local newspaper; call your union

■ **For specialists:** Get in touch with nearby technical and vocational schools; call private employment agencies; insert ads (classified or display) in your newspaper

■ **For higher-level positions:** Advertise in business, trade, or professional journals; talk over your personnel needs with a professional or trade association; contact your independent buying office

—Tip 58—

Improve your interviewing skills and techniques.

Avoid giving interviews on the run. You'll need ample time to review the employment application; to offer information about your company and the job in question; and to evaluate the candidate's merits, drawbacks, and potential contributions. For most job openings, two interviews are preferable to one. A third interview is often useful for higher positions.

Always hold an interview in a quiet room and don't permit interruptions of any kind.

Actions to Consider:

■ For a less subjective and more accurate assessment of each candidate's strengths and weaknesses, complete an objective-type rating form at the close of the interview.*

■ Lend structure to the initial interview by following a predesigned set of questions.

■ Keep the interaction on track at all times.

■ Phrase your questions so as to encourage detailed responses.

---

*To develop a useful rating form, follow this procedure:

1. On a blank sheet of paper, list such applicant attributes as business experience, communication skills, education, emotional control, enthusiasm, grooming, self-confidence—and any other traits that are important to you.

2. Set four additional columns on the page; head them up as follows:
   1—"Poor"   3—"Good"

   2—"Fair"   4—"Excellent"

3. For each applicant interviewed, check the appropriate column alongside each trait.

4. After the interview, count the number of checks you entered in the first column. Place that total at the bottom of column 1.

5. Add up the check marks in column 2, multiply that number by 2, and enter the new figure at the bottom of the second column.

6. Proceed in the same manner with columns 3 and 4, making sure to multiply the number of checks in column 3 by 3—and the number in column 4 by 4.

7. Total all amounts below the columns to arrive at an overall score for the applicant.

- Encourage the applicant to talk about the more significant contributions he or she made to former employers.

- Investigate evident omissions in the jobseeker's work history.

- Explore the applicant's reasons for having left earlier positions.

- Be alert for insights into the applicant's work attitudes, skills, talents, judgment, and ability to communicate.

- Try to assess such personality traits as drive, enthusiasm, empathy, and self-control.

—Tip 59—

Check applicants' references carefully.

Before making your decision, take the time to corroborate all significant details on the employment application. In addition, query all references given by the candidate by mail and/or telephone.

—Tip 60—

Test applicants only if necessary.

As a general rule, you should refrain from the use of tests as aids in the selection process. On occasion, however, you may need to employ some sort of performance, aptitude, or achievement test when screening candidates for skilled positions; for example: machinist, computer operator, carpenter, translator, bookkeeper, or electrician.

To avoid possible complaints from job applicants and comply with existing federal legislation, give only tests that are both valid and reliable.

—Tip 61—

If you haven't issued one as yet, prepare and distribute an employees' handbook.

See to it that every employee gets a copy of your Employees' Handbook. Ideally, this publication should offer answers to most of the questions that new hires might ask. It should contain information on the following topics:

- The history of the company (including the firm's mission and long-range objectives)

- Management organization—executives, departments and department heads, and so on

- Company policies

- Company products and/or services

- Employee compensation plan(s)

- Employee benefits, including vacation days, sick days, etc.

- Working conditions, safety and health rules, the grievance system, and other aspects of personnel administration

- Company-community relations

—Tip 62—

Devise and implement a comprehensive indoctrination program.

The curriculum for the employee indoctrination program should, for the most part, parallel the topics set forth in the earlier-mentioned Employees' Handbook. In addition, it should provide: (1) an orientation to the particular departments to which the newly hired personnel have been assigned, and (2) the new employees' duties and responsibilities.

—Tip 63—

Place every new hire on probation for thirty days.

Institute a thirty-day probationary period for every new employee. A week before the period ends, the probationer is to be evaluated by his or her immediate superior. Devise a form to aid the evaluation process.

An example of such a form appears in figure 3-2. It lists fourteen distinct criteria, each of which is followed by the numerals 1 through 4. For each criterion, the rater is to circle one number according to the following scale:

1—Poor   3—Good
2—Fair   4—Very Good

To obtain the probationer's total score on this form: (1) count the number of circles in each column, (2) enter each column's total on the appropriate line in the scoring chart at the bottom of the page, (3) multiply out each line, and (4) add up the last column in the scoring box.

Company management must determine in advance the total score needed for the successful completion of the probationary period. You might, perhaps, choose a score of 28 as the lowest acceptable score; a score below 28 would constitute grounds for dismissal. (Note that a "Fair" rating on all fourteen criteria yields a total score of 28 (14×2 points).)

In preparing your own evaluation instrument, feel free to discard any or all of the criteria shown in figure 3-2 and replace them with others of your own choosing.

TAILORING YOUR PAY PLAN(S) TO COMPANY NEEDS

Before initiating any study of your employee compensation approaches, be certain that your current program:

■ Offers your employees a reasonable standard of living.

■ Is appropriately scaled according to the level of work done.

■ Is competitive with those of similar firms.

■ Establishes a pay range for each position: a minimum starting salary and a maximum level to which the employee will eventually be raised.

—Tip 64—

Review your current employee compensation approaches.

Figure 3-2. Rating form for probationary employees

Evaluation of Probationary Employee

Name of probationer_____

Completed by_____Date_____

Acceptance of responsibility	1	2	3	4
Attendance	1	2	3	4
Communication skills	1	2	3	4
Cooperation	1	2	3	4
Courtesy	1	2	3	4
Dependability	1	2	3	4
Initiative	1	2	3	4
Interpersonal relations	1	2	3	4
Job knowledge	1	2	3	4
Job performance	1	2	3	4
Judgment	1	2	3	4
Punctuality	1	2	3	4
Resourcefulness	1	2	3	4
Self-confidence	1	2	3	4

Scoring Chart

_____ x 1 =

_____ x 2 =

_____ x 3 =

_____ x 4 =
_____

Total Score = _____

Begin your review by asking yourself such questions as:

■ What's the rationale behind the compensation program I now have in place?

■ Will the program help me reach my goals?

■ Is it possible to modify the program so that I attain my objectives sooner and/or reduce my costs?

Continue by exploring the pros and cons of the possibilities presented in the next section.

Actions to Consider:

■ Replace your weekly payroll with a semimonthly or monthly pay period.

■ Instead of issuing payroll checks, start a direct-deposit program.

■ Don't hand out bonuses for any reason other than for outstanding performance.

■ Start sales recruits on a basic training salary. After they're trained, switch to a commission-only plan buffered by an adequate, but not excessive, drawing account.

■ Pay somewhat higher commissions on sales to new accounts.

■ Provide extra incentive to employees in lower- and middle-management positions in the form of token cash awards for productivity increases.

■ Place ceilings on the amounts your salespeople can spend per diem on meals and for hotel accommodations.

■ Grant a small additional commission on sales over quota by at least 10 percent.

■ Raise the commission rate on sales of slow-moving goods.

■ Explore the pros and cons of tying commission rates to the gross margin earned, rather than to the product's selling prices.

■ Expand your use of nonmonetary incentives (awards of various types, bestowing a more favorable job title, a write-up in the firm's house organ, a larger desk or office, and so on).

■ Consider setting up an employee stock plan.

■ Change your group medical insurance plan to a program that requires employee contributions.

■ Stop providing annual medical checkups for your employees.

■ Rethink company policy on life insurance coverage, the use of company cars, and payment for college tuition.

■ One by one, review all other supplemental benefits you now offer. Retain only those that you judge most important to your employees and least costly to you.

DEVELOPING AND CONDUCTING BETTER TRAINING PROGRAMS

Training should be a continuous process and applied to company personnel at all levels. While its main objectives are to increase sales, reduce costs, and boost profits, training also helps to:

- Build morale
- Cut down on errors
- Develop supervisors and managers
- Improve job performance
- Increase productivity
- Instill healthy work attitudes
- Prepare employees for promotion
- Reduce the turnover rate
- Upgrade employee skills

—Tip 65—

Examine and improve all current training programs.

Follow this procedure when revising old and in planning new training programs:

- Determine the training needs of your employees
- Establish training objectives; list the specific benefits to be attained
- Prepare a budget for each training program
- Plan curricula for all programs
- Work out training schedules
- Set up the training facility and equipment
- Select the teaching methods to be used
- Choose the trainer or training staff
- Devise a method of evaluating the results of each program
- Devise new training programs as they are needed

Training Approaches

Among the more useful training techniques and visual aids are:

Apprenticeships	Internships
Audiocassetes	Job rotation
Case analyses	Lectures
Coaching	Movies
College courses	Programmed instruction
Conferences	Role playing
Demonstrations	Slides
Film strips	Trade association
Group discussions	presentations
In-basket exercises	Videocassettes

NINE SUGGESTIONS FOR RAISING EMPLOYEE PRODUCTIVITY

Employee motivation is the golden key to an increase in productivity. An alert management will continually seek ways to become more efficient, to move the entire organization towards a higher level of productivity, and to step up company output while holding down (or even lowering) costs at the same time.

Decades ago, Frederick Herzberg's classic studies revealed that such job factors as recognition, responsibility, growth, and advancement have a positive effect on employee motivation. Still other features of the workplace can contribute toward dissatisfaction on the job: these are company policy, working conditions, employee compensation, supervision, and the nature of the work performed.*

Over the next several sections of this chapter, we'll review some of the steps you can take to help boost productivity in your firm.

—Tip 66—

Enhance the physical work environment.

---

*See Frederick Herzberg, *Work and the Nature of Man.* (New York: Thomas Y. Crowell, 1960), pp. 71–91.

Devote some time to examining all areas of your business facility with an eye to providing your employees with a more enjoyable and more inviting workplace.

Find answers to such questions as:

- Are the premises properly illuminated all throughout?

- Do you keep the place comfortably cool in warm weather and comfortably warm during the colder months?

- Is the noise level kept under control at all times?

- Have you erected gates around or otherwise safeguarded all operating machinery?

- Have all work areas, furniture, meeting rooms, and even the lunchroom been laid out according to ergonomic principles?

- Are computer terminals equipped with glare-reduction screens and are keyboards set up so as to avoid eyestrain, carpal tunnel syndrome, or other injuries that may be caused by repetitive motion?

—Tip 67—

Stress promotion from within.

Make it company policy to seek candidates for higher-level positions from within your organization. Post any such openings on the firm's bulletin board. Offer your employees opportunities for growth and advancement to supervisory and management positions. And—publicize your "promotional ladder" in the Employees' Handbook.

—Tip 68—

Survey workforce attitudes.

For quick, though rough insights into your employees' attitudes toward both your firm and their jobs, prepare a one-page questionnaire on which only these four entries have been printed.

What I like most about this company:

What I dislike most about this company:

What I like most about my job:

What I dislike most about my job:

Be sure to leave ample space after each entry. Distribute the questionnaires to all employees.* Tell them that you expect complete honesty on their part and that they're not to sign their names. Suggest that they disguise their handwriting or print their answers so as to make identification difficult. Instruct them to drop their completed forms into the slotted box you've provided for the survey.

Figure 3-3 shows another type of survey instrument, one that's easy to apply and will provide even more useful information.

Here's how to tabulate your employees' responses:

1. Use a blank copy of the questionnaire as a worksheet for recording the information.

2. Begin with the first statement ("This is a good company to work for"). Leaf through the completed questionnaires, tallying up the check marks you find in column 1 ("Strongly Agree"). Pencil in the sum over the dash in column 1 of your record sheet.

3. Staying with the first statement, repeat the procedure with columns 2, 3, 4, and 5.

4. Go to the next statement ("My work is interesting"). Continue on as indicated above until you've entered totals in all columns for all eleven statements on the instrument.

At this juncture, a quick example may prove useful. Assume that all twenty-six of your employees have responded to the survey. After you've completed step 4 above, the first two lines on your worksheet should look something like this:

| This is a good company to work for | 6 | 14 | 4 | 2 | 0 |
| My work is interesting | 3 | 12 | 2 | 7 | 2 |

---

*If your workforce is large, try submitting the questionnaire to a random sample of employees at all levels in the organization.

Figure 3-3. Sample instrument for an employee survey

Instructions: Alongside of each phrase, place a check mark in the column that most accurately describes how you feel about it.

	Strongly Agree (1)	Agree (2)	Can't Decide (3)	Disagree (4)	Strongly Disagree (5)
This is a good company to work for					
My work is interesting					
Our company's policies are fair					
My coworkers are friendly					
There is opportunity for advancement					
Working conditions are good					
My supervisor is competent					
Management is sensitive to our needs					
This is a comfortable place to work					
Our training programs are productive					
Everyone is treated fairly					

Now, proceed to treat the worksheet data as shown below so that you can come up with a group score, or consensus:

1. Leave all figures you've entered in the first column exactly as they are.

2. Multiply all your entries in the second column by 2. Cross out your original figures and write in the new amounts.

3. Work through the remaining three columns, multiplying your figures by 3, 4, or 5 as indicated by the digits at the top of each column.

4. For each statement, add the entries across all five columns. Place the resulting sum at the end of the line and circle it.

5. Finally, divide the circled totals by the number of respondents; this will give you an "average score," or consensus for the entire group. Enter this score at the left of the statement.

After you've completed step 5, the first two lines on the worksheet should look something like this:

		28	12	8	0	
2.1 This is a good company to work for	6	14	4	2	0	(54)

		24	6	28	10	
2.7 My work is interesting	3	12	2	7	2	(71)

An average score of 3 or higher on any statement should prompt you to take swift remedial action. Scores between 2 and 3, such as those shown in the above example, indicate the need for further investigation and problem solving.

—Tip 69—

Broaden the scope of each employee's workload and encourage on-the-job growth.

Do all you can to relieve the monotonous aspects of each job. Spice things up; make work more interesting for your employees.

Actions to Consider:

■ Train employees in different types of work by rotating them both within and between departments.

■ Occasionally, assign an additional responsibility.

■ Don't keep anyone in the same job too long.

■ Create special projects that will involve group work.

■ Provide space for a company library, fill its shelves with business books and magazines, and encourage off-duty browsing.

—Tip 70—

Interview every employee who leaves.

Arrange an exit interview with every individual who leaves the company. If you possibly can, handle the interview yourself. Explore his or her reasons for leaving. Don't hesitate to ask direct questions in a friendly and open manner. You may be surprised at the wealth of information you can obtain this way. You may uncover problems caused by flawed company policies, incompetent supervision, or other organizational deficiencies.

—Tip 71—

Save thousands of dollars by implementing the following measures.

Labor costs often represent the second highest expenditure on a company's income statement, second only to the cost of goods. You can cut down on labor costs by employing one or more of the tactics suggested below.

Actions to Consider:

- Save on taxes, group health insurance, and workers' compensation insurance by hiring temporary help or leasing employees.

- Give jobseekers the opportunity to learn a skilled trade by offering apprenticeships.

- Fill temporary openings of a specialized or professional nature by appointing college seniors as summer interns—at no salary or at a token salary for the internship period.

- If you have a small business, employ 300 or fewer full-timers, and your gross receipts are $1 million or less, you can earn a tax credit of up to $5,000 for expenses you incur in providing access to disabled persons. (Ask your accountant about the Americans With Disabilities Act of 1990 and IRS Form 8826!)

- Reduce your taxes by contracting with engineers, designers, computer programmers, and other professionals to do work for you as independent contractors. (Note that the general rule for determining independent contractor status is: ". . . if you, the payer, have the right to control or direct only the results of the work and not the means and methods of accomplishing that result."*

■ Save time, effort, and money by holding teleconferences instead of meetings at hotels or restaurants.

—Tip 72—

Evaluate all employees annually.

Make it company policy to evaluate all employees once each year. Prepare an employee evaluation form, modeling it after the rating sheet for probationers that you saw in figure 3-2. Of course, you'll need to add more, and more advanced, criteria to the new form.

—Tip 73—

Maintain a high level of organizational morale at all times.

A machine will perform smoothly and almost effortlessly if all its components are in good shape and well maintained. So, too, will an organization when all employees are putting forth their best efforts and a high level of morale is sustained.

Spend some time looking over the morale-boosting measures suggested in the next section.

Actions to Consider:

■ Treat each employee as an individual.

■ Make it company policy to deal fairly and impartially with all personnel.

■ Promote an atmosphere of open, three-way communication throughout the organization.

■ Work at instilling an "owner attitude" in all employees.

■ Devise ways to upgrade employee knowledge and skills.

---

*Internal Revenue Service, "1994 Tax Guide for Small Business, *Publication 334* (Washington, D.C.: IRS, 1994), 169.

■ Request employee input when preparing labor schedules

■ Instruct all supervisors and management personnel never to criticize an employee in front of anyone else.

■ Use positive reinforcement; giving praise when deserved is great for morale.

■ Recognize and reward accomplishments.

■ Initiate a workshare (job-sharing) program.

■ Encourage employees' participation in setting goals and making decisions.

■ Keep your personnel informed about the company's current situation and any planned changes.

■ Offer flextime arrangements to interested employees.

■ Experiment with a gainsharing program.

—Tip 74—

Tone up the quality level of your supervisory staff.

Plan and institute an advanced training and skills development program for all supervisory personnel. Build into the curriculum such topics as:

■ Human relations

■ Communication (and listening)

■ Sensitivity training

■ Employee motivation

■ Conflict resolution

■ Decision making

■ Prioritizing work activities

USEFUL REFERENCES

Ambrose, Sandra and Daniel Hellmuth. *Telemarketing Skills Training Manual.* Englewood Cliffs, N.J.: Prentice-Hall, 1990.

Beach, Dale S. *Personnel: The Management of People at Work*, 6th rev. ed. New York: Macmillan, 1994.

Beck, John D.W. and Neil M. Yeager. *The Leader's Window*. New York: Wiley, 1994.

Burstiner, Irving. *The Small Business Handbook*, rev. ed. New York: Simon & Schuster, 1994.

_____. *Basic Retailing*, 2d ed. Homewood, Ill.: Irwin, 1991.

Catt, Stephen E. and Donald S. Miller. *Supervision: Working with People*, 2d ed. Homewood, Ill.: Irwin, 1991.

Donnelly, James H., James L. Gibson, and John M. Ivancevich. *Fundamentals of Management*, 7th ed. Homewood, Ill.: Irwin, 1990.

Dorio, Marc A. *Personnel Manager's Desk Book*. Englewood Cliffs, N.J.: 1989.

Hilgert, Raymond and Theo Haimann. *Supervision: Concepts and Practices of Management*, 5th ed. Cincinnati: South-Western, 1991.

Hodgetts, Richard M. and Donald F. Kuratko. *Management*, 3rd ed. San Diego, Calif.: Harcourt Brace Jovanovich, 1991.

Holton, Bill and Cher Holton. *The Manager's Short Course*. New York: Wiley, 1992.

Ivancevich, John M. and William F. Glueck. *Foundations of Personnel: Human Resource Management*. Homewood, Ill.: Irwin, 1989.

Kaliski, Burton S. and Peter F. Meggison. *Management of Administrative Office Systems*, 2d ed. San Diego: Harcourt Brace Jovanovich, 1988.

Lesikar, Raymond V. *Basic Business Communication*, 5th ed. Homewood, Ill.: Irwin, 1991.

Mosley, Donald C. et al. *Supervisory Management: The Art of Working With and Through People*, 2d ed. Cincinnati: South-Western, 1988.

Rue, Leslie W. and Lloyd L. Byars. *Management: Theory and Application*, 5th ed. Homewood, Ill.: Irwin, 1989.

Sherman, Arthur W. and George W. Bohlander. *Managing Human Resources*, 9th ed. Cincinnati: South-Western, 1992.

4/   REORGANIZE YOUR FACILITY

Requirements for the location, premises, and layout of a business facility differ from one type of enterprise to the next. The manufacturing plant, the wholesaling establishment, the retail store, and the service operation all have special needs with regard to these three essential elements. Topping the list of desirable location factors for a factory, for example, may be the availability of local labor and nearby transportation facilities. For the retail firm, the choice of a location may determine its success or demise; other factors of significance to retailers are community demographics and local competition.

EVALUATE YOUR BUSINESS LOCATION AND LAYOUT

You've occupied your place of business for a considerable period of time. Now, take an hour out of your busy schedule to review both your location and the layout of your premises.

—Tip 75—

Evaluate your location for the long term.

PROBLEM INDICATORS IN THE PRODUCTION/FACILITY AREA

Stay on the alert for any of these warning signs:

- Finding yourself tight for space (limited room for manufacturing or warehousing, selling areas, office space)

- Failing to attain production objectives

- Rising production costs

- Depleted or overloaded inventory

- Excessive downtime

- More job-lot production, fewer long production runs

- Poor coordination among production sections or between production and purchasing

- A rising scrap rate

- Too many rejects

- Decline in product quality

- Interruptions in materials flow

- Aging machinery or equipment

- Tools or equipment often missing from maintenance shop

- Evidence of poor routing, loading, or scheduling

- Increase in warehouse costs

- Paperwork piling up

- Unexpected shortages of materials, components, or supplies

- Growing number of back orders

- Too many customer returns

- Dispatching problems

- Delivery delays

- Inconsistencies in customer service

Figure 4-1 displays those aspects meriting your close attention if you hope to modify and improve your place of business.

How well suited is your business location to your needs? Can you handle continued sales growth for the foreseeable future from your current premises? Should you need to expand your facility some day, would adjacent property be available? Do you foresee substantial change in the area's demographics over the next decade that might have a deleterious effect on your operation?

Naturally, you're not about to leave your location at this point; you've invested too much time, effort, and money building it up. Someday, though, you may need to give serious thought to relocating your plant, warehouse, store, or

Figure 4-1. Facility and production aspects to target for investigation

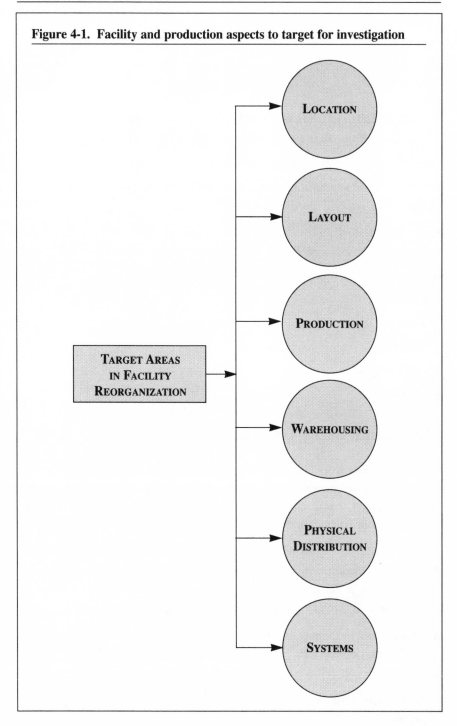

service premises. If this happens, you'll want to take into consideration many of the location factors listed in figure 4-2.

—Tip 76—

Manufacturer: Review your plant's layout and take a long, hard look at how the production area has been set up.

In addition to providing ample room for the production area, the manufacturing facility typically needs space for such functions as:

- Accounting
- Maintenance
- Personnel
- Receiving
- Sales
- Shipping
- Stockkeeping
- Warehousing

Manufacturing Operations

Space and layout requirements for the production area will vary in accordance with the kind of processing activity that goes on in the plant and with how operations are geared; that is to say, whether production is continuous or intermittent.

The major types of manufacturing activity are:

- **Analysis.** The breaking down of raw materials into their various components.
- **Assembly.** Manufacturing a new product by combining a number of sections, components, or parts.
- **Extraction.** Removing substances from materials.
- **Fabrication.** Reshaping, bending, milling, cutting, or in some other way altering the form of materials.
- **Synthesis.** Deriving new products from combining materials.
- **Transformation.** Processing materials to change them into entirely new products.

Figure 4-2. Location factors

Cost Factors:

- Cost of land
- Property costs/rental levels
- Taxes (local, state, federal)

General Factors:

- Availability of labor
- Ease of access
- Local ordinances
- Possibilities for expansion
- Quality of local services (police and fire protection, water supply)
- Transportation facilities
- Zoning regulations

Quality of Life Factors:

- Attractiveness of area
- Climate
- Cultural activities
- Houses of worship
- Housing characteristics
- Movie houses
- Public schools
- Recreational areas

Additional Factors of Importance to Retailers and Many Service Firms:

- Availability of public transportation
- Community demographics
- Compatibility of neighboring businesses
- Competition
- Extent of trading area
- Parking facilities
- Population density

Type of Production Output

Factories gear up for intermittent or flow-line production. Determine which of the three approaches below characterizes your plant:

■ **Job-lot Production.** Manufacturing products in small quantities to fulfill current orders. These are mostly custom-made items. Machine runs are short and production is intermittent. Much time is spent setting up the machines, which are often idle. Labor costs are relatively high.

   If this description matches your operation, make the progression to batch production your next goal.

■ **Batch Production.** Manufacturing goods, typically standard products, in somewhat larger quantities (batches), to fulfill in-house orders and to build up inventory against future demand. Grouping orders by product type, less frequent set-ups, longer machine runs, less idle time, and lower costs are characteristic of this production approach.

   If you're already at this stage, it's not too early to set your sights on continuous, or flow-line, production.

■ **Flow, or Flow-line, Production.** This stage represents the highest level of productivity and the pinnacle of profitability. Machines run uninterruptedly for lengthy periods of time, producing standard products. Two, and often three, different shifts may have to be staffed in order to maintain production.

—Tip 77—

Manufacturer: Review the production area layout.

Basically, there are two types of layout configurations:

■ **Process Layout.** Adopted by most small and medium-size plants, this is the typical configuration for both job and batch production. Machines are grouped according to the kind of processing that is required.

■ **Product Layout.** In this type of layout, the machinery is positioned so that a specific sequence of operations can be conducted. Generally, this is the preferred approach for flow-line production.

   Examine the layout of your production area. How are your machines set up? Have you followed a process layout or a product layout? Would it prove beneficial for you to change at this point in time from your present set-up to the other type?

—Tip 78—

Wholesale, retail, and service companies: Evaluate the layout of your premises.

Most business premises need to provide space for the same basic functions that were mentioned earlier in connection with manufacturing plants (see tip 76). For your convenience, they are repeated here:

Accounting	Sales
Maintenance	Shipping
Personnel	Stockkeeping
Receiving	Warehousing

Retail firms also need room for a storefront, outside (overhead) sign, show window(s), interior displays, and workrooms. Many service businesses have special needs that dictate their layouts; machinery, equipment, and furnishings may occupy a large part of the premises. Reception and work areas may also be needed. Examples that come readily to mind include: auto repair shops, car washes, fitness centers, beauty salons, spas, bowling alleys, restaurants, and dental labs.

Actions to Consider:

■ Make certain that all aisles are wide enough to accommodate customers, company personnel, and the passage of cartons of goods.

■ Inspect all shelving and bins to ensure that they're strong, well-installed, and properly situated.

■ Provide sufficient lighting throughout the premises to avoid accidental injuries.

■ Regularly check belts, carts, conveyors, dollies, forklifts, slides, and other equipment used to move goods and materials.

■ In the retail store, expand the selling area and cut down on nonselling space.

■ Choose a *grid layout* to maximize shopper exposure to the merchandise. To provide a more pleasant environment for leisurely shopping, change to a *free-form layout*. If you have a large, departmentalized store, consider creating a more attractive *boutique layout* by refashioning the various sections into individual shops.

- In the service operation, improve the decor of the premises and upgrade the furnishings.

- If you offer service(s) that can also be delivered by truck, go mobile—bring the facility to the customer.

- Follow the *straight-line principle* in setting out your service operation—arrange entrance(s), exit(s), machinery, and equipment so that customers can be served faster and better.

REDUCING YOUR PRODUCTION COSTS

Every single item manufactured in your plant adds some amount, however insignificant, to your operating expenses and therefore affects your income statement. Included in this figure are the costs of:

- Raw materials
- Components
- Direct labor
- Packaging
- An allocated share of overhead expenses

You can effect considerable savings by cutting down on your production costs. These savings will translate directly to higher end-of-year profits.

—Tip 79—

Streamline your production department.

Get involved researching the entire production area. Mentally divide the area into three or four sections. Study the ongoing activities within each section, one at a time, to see if you can find ways to circumvent bottlenecks, speed up production, lower costs, or put into place some other positive changes.

Actions to Consider:

- Keep machinery and equipment in top working order and schedule weekly maintenance checks. Repair or replace faulty equipment.

- Strive to build up sales to the point where you can upgrade from predominantly job-lot production to batch production (and, eventually, to flow-line production).

- Increase the number of smooth, uninterrupted machine runs by grouping orders for similar types of goods.

- Make the work area safer and make it easier for employees to detect and reject imperfect goods by providing proper lighting.

- Employ time- and work-study techniques to improve productivity.

- Initiate a study project to monitor set-up times and design ways to shorten these periods.

- Pinpoint other areas for cost savings.

- Save time by stocking component parts on or adjacent to the shop floor.

- Keep your machines running during slow periods by offering regular-line items at reduced prices.

- Outline and adopt a tight zero-defects program.

- Stress cleanliness on the shop floor and throughout the production facility.

- Maintain a comfortable room temperature during working hours.

- Analyze operations to determine if, where, and how automation can be applied to help speed up production.

- Avoid unexpected shortages in materials and components with improved inventory planning, scheduling, and routing.

- If and when incoming orders overwhelm plant capacity, turn some work over to subcontractors.

- Direct the purchasing department to institute a vendor analysis program and rate all suppliers at least once a year.

—Tip 80—

Reduce manufacturing costs by simplifying and standardizing some products.

Carefully examine each item in your product line to determine if you can reduce the number of parts or components it contains. Apply value analysis methods. Question the contribution that each part or component makes to the whole and ascertain whether or not you can replace two (or more) parts by one that serves the same function(s). Manufacturing products that are less complex will lower your cost of materials and save production time.

You can lower expenses even more by standardizing as many products as you can. Producing mostly standard goods reduces the variety of products that must be maintained in inventory and also shortens lead-time, set-up time, and machine time.

—Tip 81—

Seek improvements in other departments to lower overhead expenses.

Not only are your profits affected by your expenditures for rent, executive salaries, insurance, and other overhead costs but also by the costs of operating all other sections or departments. In addition to looking into those functions previously mentioned (accounting, maintenance, personnel, and so on), check into the purchasing department, the quality control section, and plant security.

Every function in your business needs to be examined closely. You'll find many useful suggestions for improving other areas in the remaining chapters of this book.

IDEAS FOR CUTTING WAREHOUSING AND DELIVERY EXPENSES

Storage and physical distribution are two other essential areas where firm cost control is indicated.

—Tip 82—

Review your warehousing and distribution budgets.

For effective control, draw up expense budgets quarterly for both warehousing and physical distribution. Keep on top of these budgets. At the end of each quarter, compare actuals with budgeted figures and investigate deviations.

—Tip 83—

Take steps to reduce storage costs.

Yes, you can save money in your warehouse. A few suggestions are offered in the section directly below.

Actions to Consider:

- If you haven't already done so, install a perpetual inventory control program.

- Consign your goods to a public warehouse instead of renting, buying, or building a warehouse of your own.

- Designate separate areas in the warehouse for the materials inventory, semi-processed goods, and finished goods. Draw up a map that pinpoints the location of these areas.

- In the receiving section, log in the details of each delivery as it arrives—date and time of arrival, transport company, invoice number, and so on.

- Insist that every delivery be checked thoroughly against the packing slip, bill of lading, and copy of the purchase order.

- Note all errors and damaged goods. Put in claims immediately.

- Store goods on pallets or skids to avoid the possibility of flood damage.

- Save time and reduce costs by following the straight-line principle when bringing goods into or moving them out of their assigned areas in the warehouse.

- Hold down energy expenses: replace most incandescent lamps with fluorescent lighting, upgrade to energy-efficient cooling and heating systems, and install timers to turn on and shut off outside lighting.

—Tip 84—

Reduce your distribution costs.

Traffic management's primary objective is to schedule shipments so that the goods safely reach their destinations on time and at the lowest possible cost.

A good working knowledge of the available transportation facilities is an essential asset.

Transportation Modes

For most companies, the major modes of transportation are rail, truck, air, and water. Brief comments about these four modes follow:

- **Rail.** Useful for shipping large quantities of gravel, coal, and other bulk goods; agricultural products; and livestock to destinations. Carload rates are considerably lower than less-than-carload (LTC) rates. Railroads offer special services, such as diversion in transit (changes in destination while goods are en route), pooling services, and piggyback arrangements (truck trailers placed on flatcars).

- **Truck.** Most flexible of all transportation modes, trucks are relatively fast and can deliver most everywhere. Useful for shipping expensive goods short distances. (*Note:* Using common carriers is a less costly alternative to maintaining your own trucks.)

- **Air.** The fastest mode. Useful for shipping small but expensive items, perishable goods, and other products where speed is important. Shipping costs, though, are relatively high.

- **Water.** The slowest mode of all. Least expensive method of moving low-cost bulky products. Transportation by barges on the nation's inland waterways and by ocean freighters.

In addition to the major modes discussed above, there are various transportation agencies: the U.S. Postal Service (parcel post), United Parcel Service, Federal Express, Emery Air Freight, and others.

(**Note:** For useful information relating to freight charges, refer to figure 6-2 in chapter 6, particularly to the terms F.O.B., geographic, uniform delivered, and zone pricing.)

HOW TO REVISE AND UPDATE YOUR INTERNAL SYSTEMS

One characteristic of a well-run company is an open, unimpeded, three-way communications flow. Information passes readily from top management down to the lowest rung of the organizational ladder, works its way just as freely up to the top, and quickly diffuses horizontally at all levels of the hierarchy.

To facilitate three-way communications throughout your organization, carefully review all paperwork and speed up all internal systems.

—Tip 85—

Study and improve the paperwork flow.

Conduct an exhaustive review of all internal forms currently in use. Try to improve them. Pay particular attention to purchase order blanks, sales order forms, route sheets, machine load charts, and flow process charts.

In addition, review the information flow of intracompany communications: memoranda, product information, price changes, planned promotions, advertising schedules, policy changes, and so on. To keep the staff informed, consider issuing a company newsletter or magazine on a monthly or bimonthly basis.

—Tip 86—

Check all internal systems now in place.

Examine all internal systems. Try to identify and find ways to circumvent potential bottlenecks. Devise methods for speeding up all processes.

Actions to Consider:

- Chart and review your entire order-flow system from order entry through order checking, submission for credit approval, the distribution of copies to shipping, bookkeeping, and so on.

- Install a system that will ensure the complete and accurate preparation of each bill of materials. Insist on the same precision approach in the preparation of every route sheet.

- For each lengthy production run, use critical path analysis (CPA) to determine the longest possible time the job might take. Follow up by preparing a network schedule that charts all activities that need to take place.

- Use Gantt charts to keep production personnel continually informed regarding the schedule and progress of each job.

- Improve production through work measurement and methods study.
- Computerize your inventory system and maintain continuous inventory control.
- Use universal product code (UPC) numbers, point-of-sale (POS) equipment, and scanners for more efficient inventory control and faster checkout.
- Computerize your entire bookkeeping system.

USEFUL REFERENCES

Burstiner, Irving. *The Small Business Handbook: A Comprehensive Guide to Starting and Running Your Own Business*, rev. ed. New York: Simon & Schuster, 1994.

Dilworth, James B. *Production and Operations Management*, 5th ed. New York: McGraw-Hill, 1993.

Dudick, Thomas S. *Complete Guide to Modern Warehouse Management*. Englewood Cliffs, N.J.: Prentice-Hall, 1990.

Fitch, Rodney. *Retail Design*. New York: Watson-Guptill, 1991.

Fogarty, Donald W., Thomas R. Hoffmann, and Peter W. Stonebraker. *Production and Operations Management*. Cincinnati: South-Western, 1989.

Francis, Richard L. and John A. White. *Facility Layout and Location: An Analytical Approach*. Englewood Cliffs, N.J.: Prentice-Hall, 1974.

Ghosh, Avijit and Sara L. McLafferty. *Location Strategies for Retail and Service Firms*. Lexington, Mass.: Lexington Books, 1987.

Green, William R. *The Retail Store: Design and Construction*, 2d ed. New York: Van Nostrand Reinhold, 1991.

Janson, Robert L. *Handbook of Inventory Management*. Englewood Cliffs, N.J.: Prentice-Hall, 1986.

Jones, Ken and Jim Simmons. *The Retail Environment*. New York: Routledge, 1991.

Mather, Hal. *Competitive Manufacturing*. Englewood Cliffs, N.J.: Prentice-Hall, 1988.

Meredith, Jack R. *The Management of Operations*, 4th ed. New York: Wiley, 1992.

Tompkins, James A. and John A. White. *Facilities Planning*. New York: Wiley, 1984.

Young, Allan. *Complete Plant Operations Handbook: A Guide to Cost Reduction, Quality Control and On-Time Delivery*. Englewood Cliffs, N.J.: Prentice-Hall, 1990.

5/ STRENGTHEN YOUR PRODUCT/SERVICE MIX

Today's marketing managers devote their energies to firming up those "Four P's" of the marketing mix: product, price, promotion, and place (distribution). Regarded by these professionals as the most important P of all is that first one—*product*. They believe that the most direct path to sales growth is to focus on the customer, ascertain that person's needs or wants, and then offer products (at the right prices) designed to satisfy those needs or wants.

Effective management of a company's product-service mix calls for proficiency in such areas as:

- Preparing sales forecasts
- Determining the quantities of goods and/or services needed to attain forecasted sales
- Proscribing changes within, additions to, and deletions from the firm's product line
- Developing new products and/or services
- Buying goods and/or services for resale—or purchasing raw materials, components, installations, machinery, accessory equipment, and services for internal use

PROBLEM INDICATORS IN THE PRODUCT/SERVICE AREA

You can expect eventual turmoil in the product/service management sphere if you find evidence of:

- Not meeting your sales projections
- A depleted or overloaded inventory

81

- Higher inventory carrying costs

- Too long or too short a product line

- Keeping slow-moving goods in the line long after they should have been dropped

- New-product development at a standstill

- Selling products that cannibalize other items in your line

- Staple goods frequently out-of-stock

- Shortages of materials, components, or supplies

- Increasing numbers of customer returns

To strengthen your product/service mix, begin scrutinizing each of the areas designated in figure 5-1.

A PROGRAM FOR MORE ACCURATE FORECASTS

Sales forecasts lie at the very heart of inventory planning, for you must provide enough goods to reach your sales objective.

Many companies break the year down into four seasons, forecasting sales for each season and laying their merchandise plans accordingly. Generally, this is preferable to working within a two-season context: spring-summer and fall-winter.

—Tip 87—

Fine-tune your sales forecasts.

Before attempting to forecast sales, try to gain insights into what the future may hold. Read widely and voraciously in newspapers, magazines, and trade journals in your area of business. Listen to business news on radio and TV. Get information from government reports. Peruse all internal records: company sales for the last few years, the results of past ad campaigns and sales promotions, and so on.

Try to arrive at acceptable answers to these vital questions:

1. What will our economy be like next year? Will things be better than, worse than, or on a par with this year's economy?

Figure 5-1. Product/service aspects to target for investigation

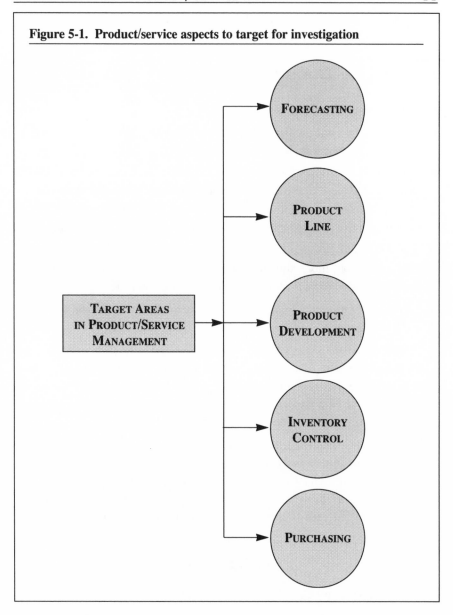

2. How will our own industry do? Will its performance parallel that of the over-all economy? If not, by what percentage do you expect it to differ?

3. Will our firm's performance match, surpass, or fare worse than the rest of our industry?

Answers to these questions will help to crystallize your thinking about company sales for next year.

Actions to Consider:

- Stay on top of significant economic trends.

- Watch the economic indicators: consumer spending, productivity, the gross national product, the prime rate, and so on.

- Tap your top executives for their estimates of next year's sales volume. Use the Delphi technique—kick back their replies with a suggestion that they reconsider their original sales projections. Resubmit their figures another time or two until you're satisfied that you have their best thinking on the matter.

- Ask your field salesforce to forecast sales for their individual territories; they're probably more knowledgeable about their customers' situations and plans for future orders than anyone else in your organization.

- Survey your customers by mail or telephone to find out what and about how much they intend to buy from you during the coming year.

- Conduct trend analysis, applying time series methods. Review your sales data for the past three to five years to find out if revenues are trending up or down or if your sales have been flat. Prepare your forecast by working with moving averages, allocating greater weight to the more recent years. (Note: Introduce a constant to smooth out the resulting curve.)

- In a chain-store operation, ask the unit managers to prepare and submit their individual sales forecasts. Total their forecasts to arrive at an estimated sales figure for the entire chain. Check that total against a management-generated forecast. Then, try to resolve any significant differences between the "bottom-up" and "top-down" forecasts through discussion with the unit managers concerned.

—Tip 88—

Translate your sales goals into precise merchandise needs.

Before you begin planning inventory requirements, you'll need to set policy regarding these aspects of merchandising:

- **Variety:** How many different lines of goods should we carry?

- **Assortment:** Within each line, how many choices should we offer?

■ **Width:** In each assortment, how many sizes, colors, styles, and/or other variants should we present?

■ **Depth:** How many pieces should we stock of each variant?

The Weeks of Supply Approach

This method is often used by distributors of staples—goods that move out steadily and in quantity. It seeks to provide sufficient stock for a number of weeks at the firm's customary rate of inventory turnover. Here's the procedure:

1. Use this first equation to calculate how many weeks of supply will be required for a specified period:

$$\text{Weeks of supply required} = \frac{\text{Number of weeks in period}}{\text{Stockturn rate for period}}$$

2. Then, calculate the amount of inventory needed at the beginning of the period (BOP) by solving this second formula:

BOP inventory needed = Weeks of supply required × Planned weekly sales

An Illustration

Let's assume that you want to keep a month's supply of goods on hand at all times. You've estimated that, during the month in question, sales will average $16,750 per week. Past records tell you that your inventory turns over 14.4 times a year. Now, counting one month as four weeks, enter "4" as the numerator of the fraction in the first equation. To obtain your stockturn rate for a single month, divide the annual turnover rate (14.4 times) by twelve; this gives you 1.2 times. Enter 1.2 as the denominator of the fraction, then work out the equation. As you can see, you need 3.3 weeks of supply.

Here's how to solve the second equation:

BOP inventory required = Weeks of supply required × Planned weekly sales
= 3.3 × $16,750 = $55,275

During the busier times of the year, you might consider raising your customary weeks-of-supply figure in order to keep more goods on hand. Contrariwise, you may want to lower the figure during slow periods.

The Basic Stock Method

This approach is useful in situations where the turnover rate runs from less than one time to as much as six times a year. The method calls for maintaining the same basic stock throughout a season and bringing in enough additional goods to cover each month's anticipated sales volume. Because demand can vary substantially during the year, the basic stock figure may be modified upward or downward at each change of season.

Here's the procedure:

1. Using the equation below, determine the average inventory to maintain throughout the season:

$$\text{Average inventory} = \frac{\text{Planned sales for season}}{\text{Stockturn rate for season}}$$

2. Estimate your average monthly sales for the season by solving this equation:

$$\text{Average monthly sales} = \frac{\text{Planned sales for season}}{\text{Number of months in season}}$$

3. Work out your basic stock as indicated below:

Basic stock = Average inventory – Average monthly sales

4. Finally, determine the beginning-of-the-month (BOM) inventory requirements for each month:

Required inventory (BOM) = Basic stock + Planned sales for month

An Example:

Given the following data, work out your inventory requirements for each of the three months:

Stockturn rate for season = 0.9 times

Planned sales:	January	$152,240
	February	169,210
	March	201,850
	Total for season	$523,300

Now, let's work out the equations together:

Step 1:

$$\text{Average stock} = \frac{\text{Planned sales for season}}{\text{Stockturn rate for season}} = \frac{\$523,300}{0.9} = \$581,444$$

Step 2:

$$\text{Average monthly sales} = \frac{\text{Planned sales for season}}{\text{Number of months in season}} = \frac{\$523,300}{3}$$

$$= \$174,433$$

Step 3:

Basic stock = Average stock − Average monthly sales = \$581,444 − \$174,433 = \$407,011

Step 4:

Required inventory, BOM = Basic stock + Planned sales for month

January BOM inventory = \$407,011 + \$152,240 = \$559,251

February BOM inventory = \$407,011 + \$169,210 = \$576,221

March BOM inventory = \$407,011 + \$201,850 = \$608,861

The Percentage Variation Approach

For rapidly moving inventories (stockturn rate of six or more times a year), many companies will rely on the percentage variation method of stocking. This approach takes into account both the average inventory maintained and projected sales. The special equation used lowers the relationship between inventory and sales so that changes in planned inventory can be made more easily.

Here is the way it works:

1. Determine the average stock you'll need for the season:

$$\text{Average stock} = \frac{\text{Planned sales for season}}{\text{Stockturn rate for season}}$$

2. Calculate the average monthly sales during the season:

$$\text{Average monthly sales} = \frac{\text{Planned sales for season}}{\text{Number of months in season}}$$

3. Work out each month's required BOM inventory:

$$\text{BOM inventory required} = \text{Average stock} \times \frac{1}{2}\left[1 + \frac{\text{Planned sales for season}}{\text{Average monthly sales}}\right]$$

An Example:

Given the following data, work out inventory requirements for each of the three months:

Stockturn rate for season = 2.7 times

Planned sales:	Month 1 =	$382,500
	Month 2 =	298,000
	Month 3 =	427,500
	Total for season =	$1,108,000

Step 1:

$$\text{Average stock} = \frac{\text{Planned sales for season}}{\text{Stockturn rate for season}} = \frac{\$1,108,000}{2.7} = \$410,370$$

Step 2:

$$\text{Average monthly sales} = \frac{\text{Planned sales for season}}{\text{Number of months in season}} = \frac{\$1,108,000}{3}$$

$$= \$369,333$$

Step 3:

$$\text{BOM inventory required} = \text{Average stock} \times \frac{1}{2}\left[1 + \frac{\text{Planned sales for month}}{\text{Average monthly sales}}\right]$$

$$= \$410,370 \times \frac{1}{2}\left[1 + \frac{\$382,500}{\$369,333}\right]$$

$$= \$410,370 \times \frac{1}{2}[1 + 1.04] = \$410,370 \times \frac{1}{2}(2.04)$$

$$= \$410,370 \times 1.02 = \$418,577$$

Now, proceed in the same manner for the balance of the season. Compute the required BOM inventory for month 2 as indicated below:

$$= \$410,370 \times \frac{1}{2}\left[1 + \frac{\$298,000}{\$369,333}\right]$$

$$= \$410,370 \times \frac{1}{2}(1.81)$$

$$= \$410,370 \times 0.905$$

$$= \$371,385$$

Here are the calculations for the BOM inventory needed for month 3:

$$= \$410,370 \times \frac{1}{2}\left[1 + \frac{\$427,500}{\$369,333}\right]$$

$$= \$410,370 \times \frac{1}{2}[2.16]$$

$$= \$410,370 \times 1.08$$

$$= \$443,200$$

Retail Reductions

Whatever method may be used for merchandise planning, retailers need to antici-
pate the effects of the usual *retail reductions* on their inventories. To compensate
for these effects, additional stock must be provided for:

■ Employee discounts

■ Customer discounts

■ Markdowns

■ Stock shortages

CONSOLIDATE AND IMPROVE YOUR PRODUCT LINE

The 80-20 Rule is a rough but useful guide for making decisions in the product
management area. Indeed, you'll find this aid works just as well in other aspects
of your business operation.

By way of illustration, here are two applications of the 80-20 Rule to a company's product line—and a third that is of value in managing a salesforce:

■ 80 percent of the products in a manufacturer's line bring in only 20 percent of
the company's sales—and contrariwise, 20 percent of the items produce about
80 percent of the firm's revenues.

■ 80 percent of the merchandise sold by a wholesaler or retailer account for
about 20 percent of the sales volume; the other 20 percent contribute 80 percent of sales.

■ 80 percent of the orders submitted by a salesforce are written by about 20 percent of the salespeople—and vice versa.

Apparently, the more products in a manufacturer's line, the greater the number of items carried by a wholesaler or retailer, and the larger the salesforce, the more the 80-20 Rule applies.

Keep the 80-20 Rule in mind as you start delving into the product area.

—Tip 89—

Track the movement of every product in your line.

Monitor your product line continually. For optimum results, computerize the process. If you're not already using stockkeeping unit numbers (SKUs), assign code numbers to all your products. Reserve the first two digits of the code for identifying the category to which the product belongs; assign the next two to four digits to the item itself, and use the remaining digits to describe the different colors, sizes, styles, or other variants.

Maintain accurate records of product movement throughout the year. Record, preferably by computer, the following information:

- Code number
- Item description
- Unit cost
- Unit selling price
- Gross margin dollars earned per unit
- Quantity sold
- Sales dollars generated

—Tip 90—

Conduct an annual performance review of your entire product/service line.

Shortly after the close of each year, prepare two distinct lists from your product-sales data: (1) the total number of units sold per item, and (2) the total sales dollars generated per item. Arrange each list in descending order from best to poorest seller. Make a computer printout of both lists, arranged first by categories of goods and then by individual items.

—Tip 91—

Redflag, then evaluate, the lowest 20 percent on each list.

Cross-match the low performers to find out which products appear toward the bottom of both lists. One by one, subject each to thoughtful examination. Before deciding to drop an item from your line, try to find answers to such questions as:

- To what can we attribute its lackluster performance?
- Was it priced too high? Too low?
- Were its sales affected negatively by some competitive item in our line?
- How much more would we have sold if we had promoted it properly?
- Is the item in the decline stage of its product life cycle?
- Can we redesign the product to make it more salable?
- Can we locate a hitherto untapped market for the product?

After due deliberation, start building a list of the items to be dropped from the line.

—Tip 92—

Replace discontinued products with new items that offer greater sales potential.

To locate promising new products, be sure to:

- Watch the marketplace
- Read trade and business periodicals
- Check competitors' offerings
- Query your suppliers
- Visit showrooms and peruse distributors' catalogs
- Contact your buying office
- Invent new items (See the next section!)

GENERATE DOZENS OF NEW PRODUCT/SERVICE IDEAS WITH THESE SIMPLE CREATIVITY TECHNIQUES

To ensure your company's continued success, set up an effective internal system for the development of new products. As you no doubt realize, locating ideas for new items will be the most difficult part of the program.

The five phases in the product-development process are:

- **Idea production:** gathering and/or generating ideas for new products or services

- **Screening:** choosing the more promising concepts and discarding (or improving) the balance.

- **Development:** converting the idea into reality—all packaged, priced, and positioned.

- **Market testing**

- **Product rollout**

Yes, launching a new product can be very costly. For that very reason, many manufacturers prefer playing "follow the leader," copying the successful products of other companies rather than originating new ones. If, however, you want your organization to last for decades, you'll need to produce an occasional new item. And, who knows? Perhaps, someday, one of your innovations may bring in a million dollars or more.

—Tip 93—

Form a new idea production team.

Put together your own special task force to generate ideas for new products. Invite from five to seven employees to serve on the team. Enjoy the benefits of varied backgrounds, experience, and points of view by drawing the team members from different areas of your enterprise: production, quality control, finance, marketing, personnel, promotion, distribution, sales, and so on.

Keep in mind that the prestige associated with being invited to participate can be great for team morale!

Once the task force has been trained and is ready for action, there's little need to meet more often than once a week for an hour or two.

—Tip 94—

Energize the team members by teaching them how to brainstorm.

Brainstorming is a powerful problem-solving technique that can produce ideas by the bucketful. No more than twenty minutes of preparation are required before your team will be ready to tackle its first problem. And—its output may astound you!

Make a game of the procedure. Establish a relaxed atmosphere, an atmosphere of acceptance in which participants are encouraged to free their imaginations and, without hesitation, articulate as many ideas as they can think of without fear of criticism. (*Note:* For more information on this and other creative thinking techniques, refer to the classic work by Alex Osborn, the "father of brainstorming."*

Sessions are typically short, usually lasting no more than 20 or 25 minutes. Keep a tape recorder on hand and running because, at times, ideas will flow so quickly that not even the ablest stenotypist can record them.

After the session, a typed list of the team's output is prepared from the tape. Copies are sent to all participants, along with a memo suggesting that they look over the list and add any new thoughts that may occur to them. Often, the original list will grow in size by 10 percent to as much as 40 percent and more.

Of course, all the ideas will still need to be evaluated. A useful rating procedure is discussed later on in the chapter, under Tip 97.

Incidentally, brainstorming can be and is used by many firms not only to create new products but also to find solutions to many kinds of business problems.

—Tip 95—

Show the team how to produce dozens of ideas *via* word association.

We borrow from the psychologist's world for this approach, wielding simple words as devices to stimulate our mental processes and generate new concepts by association. Begin using the technique by listing a minimum of twenty-five

---

*Alex F. Osborn, *Applied Imagination*, 3rd rev. ed. (New York: Charles Scribner's Sons, 1963).

common nouns on a sheet of paper. You then start "mining" the list, that is to say, attempting to think up other words that are somehow linked in your mind to each noun you've written down.

Using word association can be a fun challenge. Spend half an hour practicing the method with the aid of the sample list in figure 5-2. (However, feel free thereafter to build your own list of nouns for idea production.)

To illustrate the procedure, assume that you're a toy manufacturer and you wish to expand your present product line.

Begin by tackling the first word listed in Figure 5-2: *apple*. Using free association, you may well encounter any or all of the following (along with others, of course):

round	oranges	pancakes
red	pears	jelly apple
green	juice	Garden of Eden
Apple computer	pie	Adam and Eve
tree	core	serpent
blossoms	worms	fritters
leaves	fishing	cider
branch	the Big Apple	caramel-coated apple
monkey	apple butter	

Try to visualize each association as it comes up. Can you see it? Feel or taste it? Smell it? Hear it? See if you can abstract some quality or feature from each association and direct your thoughts toward new toy concepts.

While visualizing the first four words on the list, you may come up with suggestions somewhat like these (or totally different ones):

Round:	beach or tennis balls, marbles, push or pull toys with wheels, Frisbees, hoops, globes, boomerangs, flying saucers, skateboards, gyroscopes, model kits, golf clubs
Red, Green:	crayons, paints and paint sets, artists' palettes, coloring books, signal lights for train sets, flashlights, producing other toys in the line in red or green (or other colors), an operating toy lighthouse
Apple Computer:	toy computers that flash words and/or pictures on a screen, computerized toys that talk or make sounds, electronic keyboards that play music, computer games, toy telephones, remote-controlled trucks and planes

---

Figure 5-2. Sample list for generating ideas by word association

---

apple	flower	machine	spoon
artist	gate	mountain	tire
ball	grapes	ox	train
beach	holiday	oyster	umbrella
car	horoscope	party	uncle
church	insect	plant	valley
dance	judge	queen	watch
dominoes	kangaroo	radio	wire
electricity	kitchen	ring	youth
fish	ladder	shop	zoo

Tree: board games with jungle settings, wooden figures, plush monkeys or other animals, jigsaw puzzles bearing nature scenes, puppets, miniature artificial plants, dollhouses

If you find it too difficult to generate associations with any word on your list, just skip over it to the next one. More likely than not, you'll come up with at least twenty-five toy ideas before you're halfway through your list!

—Tip 96—

Add the feature-substitution method to the team's repertoire of creativity techniques.

The feature-substitution technique can be helpful for both planning changes in existing products and generating ideas for entirely new products. Here's how to use the method:

1. Choose a product from your line. On a worksheet similar to the form in figure 5-3, enter the product's name where indicated at the top of the sheet. (*Note:* For demonstration purposes, let's assume that you're a giftwares manufacturer and you wish to expand your present product line. The line item you've selected to initiate the process is a silver tray for serving fruit.)

2. Under the appropriate column heads, briefly describe the product's main qualities or features—and then put the item back in stock.

3. In the next section ("Other Choices") and below the second double line, list in each column between ten and twenty alternatives—features or qualities that are NOT FOUND AT ALL in the original product. (Think of many different products and list their main characteristics.)

4. To add new variants to the product line, substitute one or more of the alternative choices for one or more of the original features.

Working with only the first column in figure 5-3, you'll have up to fifteen variants (different shapes of the same silver serving tray) available for inclusion in your line. With the first two columns (shapes and size), you can choose from some 225 (15 × 15) possible combinations. Moreover, as you bring additional columns into the picture, the possibilities expand dramatically:

Number of Columns	Number of Combinations
3	3,375
4	50,625
5	759,375

Many of the product ideas you generate may, of course, be poor, unattractive, or downright old hat. This isn't at all important. If we apply the normal curve concept to any batch of 100 ideas, you're likely to discover two or three that are really terrific and another 12 to 14 that are well above average.

—Tip 97—

Select the more promising concepts with the aid of a simple rating form.

Whatever the techniques used to gather your idea lists, you'll need to separate the wheat from the chaff. Use a form like the one displayed in figure 5-4. In the first column, enter brief descriptions of all the ideas you've accumulated. Then go back to the first idea on the sheet and rate it in light of each criterion indicated at the top of the page. Use this elementary scale in your ratings:

0 = Poor	2 = Good
1 = Fair	3 = Very good

Weights for the rating form in figure 5-4 were, of course, chosen arbitrarily. Each organization will need to select criteria that are important to its operation and assign appropriate weights to them.

Figure 5-3. Feature substitution worksheet

Product: Serving Tray

Shape	*Size*	*Color*	*Material*	*Use*
Oval	11" x 17"	Silver	Silver mesh	To serve fruit in

Other Choices

Shape	Size	Color	Material	Use
flat	4-1/2 inches	red	rubber	to wear
square	16 inches	nile green	plastic	to build with
pentagonal	2 feet	yellow	wood	to sit on
triangular	8" × 12'	blue	paper	to illuminate
ring-shaped	1-1/4 yards	orange	copper	to play with
round	1/2 meter	purple	steel	to decorate
oblong	4' × 8"	black	cloth	to sip through
conical	tiny	gold	tin	to fasten with
spherical	small	white	glass	to talk through
octagonal	medium-sized	multicolored	ceramic	to ride in
hexagonal	large	red with blue polka dots	bronze	to protect with
pyramidal	huge	orange and blue stripes	gold	to climb on
L-shaped	5" × 8" × 11"	clear	wool	to catch with
T-shaped	1' × 2-3/4'	yellow-green	liquid	to eat with
curved	26" × 42"	pink	marble	to support

As soon as you've finished rating all ideas, return to the first one. Now you need to take the weights into account; here's how to go about it:

1. Multiply your first rating by the weight indicated atop the first column. (*Note:* In the sample chart shown in figure 5-4, "Cost" is the criterion for the first column and it carries a weight of 5X.)

2. Cross out your original entry and write the new, weighted score above it.

3. Work across the chart, following the same procedure with all other "Criteria" columns and weights.

4. Total all weighted scores for idea 1 and enter this sum in the last column (under "Score").

5. Continue in the same manner as outlined above until all ideas have been properly scored.

6. Select those ideas that scored high on the rating form for further analysis and development.

Figure 5-4. Idea rating chart

				Criteria			
(Weights)	Cost (5X)	Time Frame (2X)	Sales Potential (5X)	Compatibility with Line (2X)	Effect on Company (3X)	Existing Competition (2X)	SCORE
Idea Summaries:							
1. (short description)	5 / 1	4 / 2	10 / 2	6 / 3	3 / 1	2 / 1	30
2. (short description)	0 / 0	4 / 2	10 / 2	2 / 1	6 / 2	2 / 1	24
3. (short description)	10 / 2	2 / 1	15 / 3	6 / 3	6 / 2	4 / 2	43
4.							
5.							
6.							
7.			*****				
25.							

MEASURES FOR TIGHTENING UP ON INVENTORY CONTROL

For most companies, inventory represents a major financial commitment. No doubt, you're well aware of the costs of maintaining an inventory. There are, however, two other costs that we seldom think about:

- **The cost of frozen money.** Any gains you might have enjoyed had you bought stocks or bonds, opened certificates of deposit, or invested in real estate instead of having allocated so much of your capital to inventory.

- **Opportunity cost.** Potential gains you may have missed out on because you tied up so much money in inventory that you lacked the funds needed to upgrade or replace machinery, hire more salespeople, advertise more often, or take advantage of some other opportunity that cropped up.

—Tip 98—

Lower your inventory carrying costs.

Maintaining an inventory can add considerably to your operating expenses. In addition to paying for storage and insurance, you'll need to allocate some percentage of your overhead (rent, utilities, and so on) to inventory maintenance. You may also incur losses due to product damage or spoilage.

Avoid excessive inventory carrying costs by keeping your stock lean and tight all year long.

—Tip 99—

Install an efficient inventory control system.

To meet the needs of both your plant and your customers, an effective inventory control system must be in place. Set up a perpetual inventory program. Establish minimum and maximum levels for every item in your line. When reordering, keep lead time in mind. Use reserve stocks strategically.

You may be able to ascertain the average inventory requirements of firms similar to yours by contacting your trade association or Dun & Bradstreet. For comparison purposes, consult the informative *Annual Statement Studies.** It con-

---

*Published by Robert Morris Associates, the national association of bank loan and credit officers. The address is: 1 Liberty Place, Philadelphia, PA 19103.

tains summaries of operating results for many types of business, arranged by Standard Industrial Classification (SIC) number. Expressed as percentages of net sales are such data as the cost of sales, gross profit, operating expenses, and inventory turnover rate.

—Tip 100—

Distributors: Ease your stocking problems with an automatic fill-in system for staples.

An automatic replenishment system for reordering staple merchandise can be most helpful. We recommend this system, based on the equation: $O = [A + B] \times W - I$

Here's what the terms represent:

O = Quantity to order

A = Number of weeks between inventory counts

B = Number of weeks that elapse from order placement to receipt of the goods into the ready stock.

W = Average number of units sold per week

I = Number of units in stock at reorder time plus the amount that may be due in from any prior order(s)

An Illustration:

You've just taken monthly inventory and may need to order more of item X. You've counted 214 units on hand and there are none on order. From personal experience, you know that about three weeks will go by before the shipment will arrive and be made ready for sale. On average, you move about 76 units of item X each week. How many should you order?

Let's begin working this out by filling in the "knowns," as follows:

A = 4   (Note: When inventory is taken monthly, we list the number of weeks as 4.)

B = 3

W = 76

I = 214

Now to solve the equation:

$$O = [A + B] \times W - I$$
$$= [4 + 3] \times 76 - 214$$
$$= 7 \times 76 - 214$$
$$= 532 - 214$$
$$= 318$$

As you see, you should order an additional 318 pieces. (Of course, if the item is sold only by the dozen, you'll need to order either 26 or 27 dozen.)

—Tip 101—

Eliminate most stockouts by adding a safety reserve.

The equation for the automatic fill-in system may be refined to avoid unexpected stockouts by adding one more term ("SS") for the reserve, or "safety stock."

The equation then becomes:

$$O = [A + B] \times W - I + SS$$

To calculate the amount of safety stock needed to avoid out-of-stocks approximately 95 percent of the time, bring the following formula into play:

$$SS = 2.3\sqrt{[A + B] \times W}$$

Now, let's borrow the data from the illustration that precedes Tip 101 and compute the amount of safety stock needed in that situation:

$$SS = 2.3\sqrt{[4 + 3] \times 76}$$
$$= 2.3\sqrt{7 \times 76}$$
$$= 2.3\sqrt{532}$$
$$= 2.3 \times 23.1$$
$$= 53$$

Purchasing another 53 pieces of item X will bring your total order to 371 units (or 31 dozen, as the case may be).

—Tip 102—

Work up model stocks for fashion merchandise, seasonal goods, and other nonstaples.

An automatic replenishment system is of no value for reordering nonstaple goods. These do not follow the same sales patterns we observe in staple merchandise.

For seasonal items, fashion goods, and other nonstaple goods you'll need to prepare, well in advance, a **model stock** for each season. Indeed, you're better off working up two or three of these inventory planning guides per season; for example: early-, mid-, and late-season model inventories.

Organize each model stock by classification, selling price, style, size, color, and other selection factors.

FOUR GUIDELINES FOR BETTER BUYING

Both the purchasing agent and the buyer of goods and/or services for resale hold complex, even demanding positions. Among their more important challenges are:

- Studying the market continually

- Identifying significant trends

- Determining customers' needs and wants

- Locating sources that can supply the required goods

- Projecting the types and quantities of goods needed to attain forecasted sales

- Selecting goods customers will buy

- Negotiating prices, terms, and conditions with suppliers

- Issuing purchase orders

- Receiving, checking, and assigning incoming goods to warehouse, ready stock, and selling areas

- Keeping accurate inventory records

—Tip 103—

Keep up with what's happening in your industry by joining a trade association.

Trade associations can be found in just about every industry and trade. These active organizations furnish all sorts of useful information to their member firms: industry news, economic analyses and trends, descriptions of new products, new sources of supply, comparative financial data, and so on. Frequently, they also provide marketing advice, accounting aid, promotional guidance, group insurance plans, and other services. Many maintain a close liaison with legislators to promote legislation favorable to their client companies.

Consult the *Encyclopedia of Associations** at your local library for the names, addresses, and telephone numbers of trade associations in your field of endeavor.

—Tip 104—

Link up with a buying group.

"In union, there is strength." So goes the old adage. Whether you're an independent retailer or own a chain of stores, you'll benefit if you combine forces with one or more other companies in the same line of trade. Because of its greater purchasing power, a buying group can wield more clout. You'll pay less for your goods and be offered better terms. You may even receive, along with other promotional deals, some cooperative advertising money.

In fields such as hardware, foods, and drugs, wholesaler-sponsored voluntary chains and retailer cooperatives have been quite successful and are open to new members.

---

*Published by Gale Research, Inc. of Detroit.

—Tip 105—

Retailers: Enlist the services of an independent buying office.

If you're a retailer who is situated far from Manhattan, Chicago, or Los Angeles, give serious consideration to joining an independent buying office. Organizations of this type employ experienced buyers who constantly scour the marketplace for new merchandise and new suppliers. This move will save you the expense of making trips to a major market center and the cost of maintaining a buyer on your staff. These offices service retailers in fields such as apparel, appliances, furniture, hardware, soft goods, and others. Your buying office will:

- Send you information about fashion trends, new products, suppliers, price changes, special promotions, and so on

- Provide office space and arrange appointments with vendors for you when you're able to get to town

- Schedule trips to vendors' showrooms for you

- Run an occasional fashion clinic

- Advise you on inventory management

- Help you locate retail merchandisers and managerial personnel

---

—Tip 106—

Improve your purchasing practices.

Put some time aside to think about your current purchasing procedures. You'll be surprised at how much improvement you may be able to effect.

Actions to Consider:

- Monitor inventory movement continually.

- Keep abreast of plant requirements for raw materials, components, and supplies.

- Before placing an order, find out if the vendor carries product liability insurance or accepts responsibility for product safety.

- Whenever possible, buy directly from the manufacturer or producer instead of from distributors.

- Devise and install an efficient vendor evaluation system.

- Keep your inventory tight by buying "hand-to-mouth" (ordering frequently in small quantities).

- When purchasing goods that are in heavy and continuous demand, contract for at least a six-month or one-year supply.

- Ask for quantity discounts.

- Use caution when buying brand-new products; order them in limited quantities until you see how well they move.

- Increase your inventory of items in the growth stage of their life cycles and add more sizes, colors, styles, and/or other variants.

- When ordering mature products, seek better terms and more promotional aid.

- Spot slow-moving goods early on and begin phasing them out of the line.

- Inquire about the availability of cooperative advertising funds and other promotional support.

- Devise and install an efficient vendor evaluation system.

- Request that your goods be prepriced before they're shipped.

- Sell off slow-moving goods and excess inventory at substantial discounts or donate them to charities.

- Attend government auctions to find low-priced machinery, equipment, and vehicles.

- Before purchasing job lots or closeout merchandise, mentally sort the goods into two separate lots: (1) those you'll be able to move at your regular selling prices, and (2) those you'll have to mark down. Calculate the sales dollars you'll most likely earn on each lot, total the two figures, and decide whether or not you'll net your customary gross margin return on the purchase.

- Check the advantages and disadvantages of bartering your goods and/or services for their equivalent value in the goods and/or services of other companies.

USEFUL REFERENCES

Burstiner, Irving. *Basic Retailing*, 2d ed. Homewood, Ill.: Irwin, 1991.
————. *Start and Run Your Own Profitable Service Business*. Englewood Cliffs, N.J.: Prentice Hall, 1993.

————. *The Small Business Handbook*, rev. ed. New York: Simon & Schuster, 1994.

Clark, Charles, *Brainstorming: How to Create Successful Ideas*. North Hollywood, Calif.: Wilshire, 1989.

Diamond, Jay and Gerald Pintel. *Retail Buying*, 4th ed. Englewood Cliffs, N.J.: Prentice-Hall, 1992.

Janson, R. *Handbook of Inventory Management*. Englewood Cliffs, N.J.: Prentice-Hall, 1986.

Kotler, Philip and Paul N. Bloom. *Marketing Professional Services*. Englewood Cliffs, N.J.: Prentice-Hall, 1984.

Levy, Michael and Barton A. Weitz. *Retailing Management*. Homewood, Ill.: Irwin, 1992.

Lovelock, Christopher H. *Services Marketing*, 2d ed. Englewood Cliffs, N.J.: Prentice-Hall, 1990.

Minichiello, Robert. *Retail Merchandising and Control*. Homewood, Ill.: Irwin, 1990.

Moore, Bill and Edgar Pessemier. *Product Planning and Management*. New York: McGraw-Hill, 1992.

Shuch, Milton L. *Retail Buying and Merchandising*. Englewood Cliffs, N.J.: Prentice-Hall, 1988.

Stone, Kenneth E. *Competing with the Retail Giants: How to Survive in the New Retail Landscape*. New York: Wiley, 1994.

6/ REFINE AND POLISH YOUR PRICING PRACTICES

Pricing is a significant, and quite intricate, element in a firm's marketing mix. Pricing competency can lead a business to prosper; poor judgment and pricing errors can propel an enterprise toward bankruptcy. All too often, sellers set prices according to what they believe their products or services are worth or to what they think buyers will pay for them.

Pricing decisions are best made by following a simple four-step procedure:

1. Select your pricing objective(s).

2. Formulate a basic pricing policy.

3. Decide on your main pricing approach.

4. Price the goods or services.

PROBLEM INDICATORS IN THE PRICING AREA

If symptoms such as those listed below have been plaguing your operation, you'll need to investigate and evaluate your pricing approaches, policies, and tactics.

■ Losing customers to competitors who offer lower prices

■ A weakening share of market

■ Level or falling sales, or sales revenues that have been growing too slowly

■ Failing to reach your targeted return-on-investment

■ Frequent buying errors

■ Excessive shipping costs

■ Having to take too many markdowns

■ Earning a gross margin percentage that is well below average for your type of business

■ Promotions that lower the selling prices on some products and slow down the sales of other items in the line.

Get started on improving your pricing procedures by examining those areas targeted in figure 6-1.

FACTORS THAT AFFECT PRICING DECISIONS

Effective price administration requires the careful consideration of various influences that lie within or outside of the business organization.

Among the internal factors that affect the pricing area are the:

■ Cost of the product/service

■ Financial status of the business

■ Location of the business

■ Pricing objective(s)

■ Product/service attributes

■ Share of market enjoyed by the company

■ Stage of the product/service life cycle

Some of the external factors that influence price-setting are the:

■ Locations of buyers

■ Competition

■ Customers (consumers, organizational buyers)

■ Economic climate

■ Legal environment

■ Leval of demand for the product/service

■ Participants in the marketing channels of distribution

■ The price-quality relationship

Figure 6-1. Pricing aspects to target for investigation

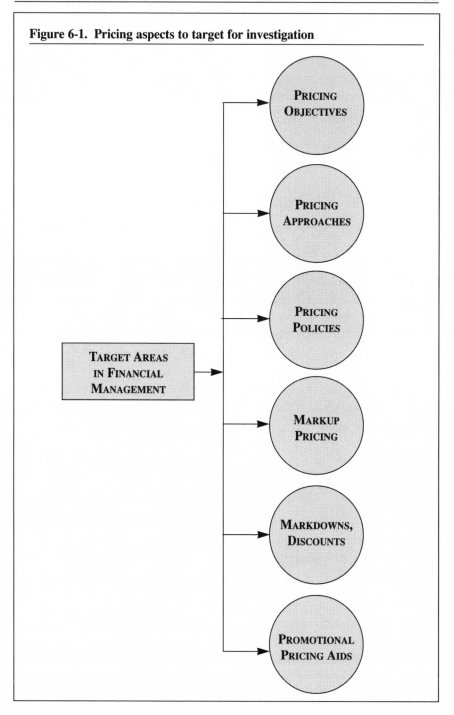

CHOOSING PRICING OBJECTIVES

Be sure to agree on the precise objective(s) you want to attain before attempting any planning whatsoever in the pricing area. Two major classes of pricing objectives are commonly seen in the business world: those linked to sales revenues and those tied to company profits.

—Tip 107—

Select and clarify your pricing objective(s).

Among the more common pricing objectives based on sales are: increasing the firm's share of market, raising current sales levels by a predetermined percentage, or producing the highest possible revenues as quickly as possible.

Objectives linked to profits include target pricing (seeking a specified profit margin), target ROI (return-on-investment) pricing (tying the desired profit percentage to the company's investment), and profit maximization (trying to end up with the highest profit percentage attainable).

There's also the far less common "status-quo" pricing objective, adopted by an occasional management that's satisfied with its current financial picture (sales *and* profits) and wants to keep it that way.

CUSTOMARY PRICE-SETTING APPROACHES

Two important questions need to be asked before management tackles the task of setting prices on company goods and/or services; both questions involve the firm's marketing philosophy:

1. Shall we set our prices *lower than, on a par with*, or *higher than* those of our competitors?

2. Shall we adopt a *penetration pricing* or a *price skimming* approach? (*Note:* If we decide on the first approach, we'll place attractively low prices on our goods and/or services so that we can penetrate the market quickly and obtain wide distribution; if we follow the latter strategy, we'll place above-average prices on our goods and/or services in order to maximize per-unit profit even though this will reduce demand considerably.

Price-setting Methods

The two most popular approaches to setting prices are cost-plus pricing and target-return pricing.

Cost-plus Pricing: The procedure in cost-plus pricing involves two steps: (1) ascertaining the product's total cost (for materials, labor, and a percentage of overhead expenses), and (2) adding to this sum the amount of profit that management would like to earn. (*Note:* Marginal, or contribution-margin, pricing is a variation of full-cost pricing.) Companies that use this approach are willing to take less of a profit and offer their goods and/or services at prices that are lower than their regular selling prices. This often happens when a firm finds itself with excess, unused capacity or when it's looking for additional business. Though the profit may be smaller than usual, it does contribute towards the company's overhead expenses.

Target Pricing: This approach involves choosing a price designed to yield a desired profit margin. The equation used to establish this price is:

$$\text{Price} = \frac{\text{Fixed costs} + \text{Variable costs} + \text{Profit}}{\text{Number of units produced}}$$

As mentioned earlier, target ROI (return-on-investment) pricing is a variation of this approach.

For a listing and brief explanations of other common pricing terms, see figure 6-2.

—Tip 108—

Learn how to conduct breakeven analysis.

Breakeven analysis is a helpful tool for ascertaining how many units of a given product must be sold at various selling prices in order for you to reach your *breakeven point*. That's the point at which total revenues equal total costs and at which you'll neither gain nor lose one red cent.

To find out how many units of any product must be sold at a particular price in order to break even, use this handy equation:

$$\text{Breakeven point (in units)} = \frac{\text{Total fixed costs}}{\text{Price} - \text{Variable costs per unit}}$$

An Illustration: Given the following information, let's find out what our breakeven point would be for product A if we offer it for sale at $25 per unit:

Figure 6-2. Pricing terms

Bait pricing. A dishonest tactic whereby a retailer promotes a popular product at a sharply reduced price in order to draw shoppers into the store. The retailer then attempts to switch the prospective buyer to another similar, but more expensive, article of merchandise.

Comparative pricing. A deceptive tactic used by a retail firm to persuade shoppers that its selling prices are well below the prices they would have to pay at competitive outlets, or that the merchandise has been marked down one or more times.

F.O.B.-factory pricing. In this approach, the manufacturer quotes a price that includes the cost of placing the outgoing shipment on board a carrier at the plant; thereafter, the buyer is to assume responsibility for subsequent freight charges to the destination point. (The initials F.O.B. stand for "free on board.")

Freight absorption pricing. A pricing method used by firms so eager for business that they're willing to pay some or all of the freight costs.

Geographic pricing. This category embraces several pricing methods tied to the location of sellers and/or buyers, such as F.O.B. factory, uniform delivered, and zone pricing.

Going-rate pricing. A pricing method of setting selling prices that are equal to the prices charged by competitors without much concern for product cost or demand considerations.

Leader pricing. This promotional pricing strategy is designed to bring many shoppers into a store. The retailer offers a popular, usually well-advertised item at a drastically reduced price, so that shoppers readily perceive the offer as an attractive bargain.

Loss leader pricing. This tactic is similar to leader pricing except that the retailer offers to sell the product at a price that is below its actual cost. Occasionally, a company may be tempted to promote an offer of this type to raise cash quickly or to sell off excess inventory. This tactic is considered illegal in many states (where a minimum markup floor must be followed).

Multi-unit pricing. To stimulate product sales, a company may offer to sell two, three, or more of the same item at a discounted price that's substantially lower than what customers would be charged if they purchased the same number of items individually.

Odd pricing. Assigning selling prices that end in odd, instead of even, figures in the belief that customers will think that the goods or services are being offered at sale or bargain prices.

Penetration pricing. A marketing strategy whereby a company chooses to affix a low selling price to a new product in order to move out inventory rapidly and in quantity.

Prestige pricing. Deliberately setting selling prices that are higher than those of competitive firms in order to attract those shoppers who seek goods of better quality or who are status conscious.

Price lining. Dividing a product class into two or more distinct groups based on product cost, quality, style, and/or other attributes and then pricing each group accordingly. This approach facilitates consumer choice and makes it easy for the retailer to satisfy customers and "trade up" some of them to a higher-priced version.

Figure 6-2. Continued

Price skimming. A policy decision that calls for placing a relatively high selling price on a new product, perhaps as a means of recouping the innovative company's investment quickly or to maximize early profits for some other reason.

Psychological pricing. A category of pricing techniques designed to appeal to shoppers' emotions and preferences. Comparative, odd, leader, and prestige pricing are examples.

Uniform delivered pricing. A company that decides on this approach will calculate its average cost of freight, add that amount to its customary selling prices, and then offer to deliver the goods at the new inclusive prices to any and all buyers, wherever they may be located.

Unit pricing. To facilitate shopper decision making, the retailer posts the cost per pound or other unit of measurement along with the regular selling price of the product.

Variable pricing. A flexible pricing policy whereby the final purchase price of a product is decided through negotiation between buyer and seller.

Zone pricing. A company that uses this approach divides its market into two or more zones; all buyers within each zone have to pay the same price; those in more distant zones are charged higher prices. (*Note:* Zone pricing is used by some manufacturers and, of course, by the U.S. Postal Service in connection with parcel post.)

Total fixed costs—$460,000

Variable costs per unit—$9

We fill in the terms and then solve the equation:

$$\text{Breakeven point (in units)} = \frac{\$460,000}{\$25 - \$9}$$

$$= \frac{\$460,000}{\$16}$$

$$= 28,750 \text{ units}$$

Wholesale, retail, and service companies can readily determine the sales volume they need to reach the breakeven point with the aid of this equation:

$$\text{Breakeven point (in dollars)} = \frac{\text{Total fixed expenses } + \text{ Total variable expenses}}{\text{Gross margin percentage of sales}}$$

An Illustration: An independent retailer has come up with the following projections for a new store unit under consideration:

Total fixed expenses = $236,450

Total variable expenses = $45,700

Gross margin percentage of sales = 42%

To determine the sales volume needed for the store to break even for its first year in business, the merchant solves the problem in the following fashion:

$$\text{Breakeven point (in dollars)} = \frac{\$236,450 + \$45,700}{0.42}$$

$$= \frac{\$282,150}{0.42}$$

$$= \$671,786$$

—Tip 109—

When setting prices, keep price elasticity of demand in mind.

Most goods in the marketplace are price-elastic, that is to say, lowering the selling price usually results in an increase in the quantity demanded—and vice versa. Before deciding on how to price their products, many companies will explore this relationship between price and demand by estimating the quantities that are likely to be purchased at each of several selling prices.

The basic equation for calculating price elasticity is:

$$\text{Price Elasticity} = \frac{\text{Percent change in quantity}}{\text{Percent change in price}}$$

MASTERING MARKUP PRICING

In markup pricing, a selling price is determined by following a two-step procedure: (1) ascertain the total cost of producing or acquiring the product or service, and then (2) add to that amount the desired margin of profit. Despite the simplicity of this cost-plus approach and its usefulness in setting prices, many businesspeople remain somewhat confused over working with markups.

—Tip 110—

Get acquainted with the basic markup equation.

The basic equation for determining the selling price to place on an individual item is:

Price = Cost + Markup

Or put more simply:

P = C + MU

Given any two of the three terms, you can readily find the third and missing term with the aid of these variations of the basic equation:

C = P – MU (Cost = Price – Markup)

MU = P – C (Markup = Price – Cost)

—Tip 111—

Determine the markup percentage you need to give you the profit margin you want.

Markups can be based on either cost or selling price. Generally, manufacturers tie their markups to cost-of-goods figures, while those merchants who work with the retail method of inventory valuation base their markups on selling prices.

Either way, markup percentages can be calculated readily with the aid of the equations indicated below:

$$\text{Markup percentage on cost} = \frac{\text{Markup (in dollars and cents)}}{\text{Cost}} \times 100\%$$

$$\text{Markup percentage on retail selling price} = \frac{\text{Markup (in dollars and cents)}}{\text{Retail selling price}} \times 100\%$$

An Illustration: A company determines that its manufacturing cost per unit of product A amounts to $3.46. The firm's policy is to sell its goods to wholesalers at prices equivalent to triple their cost. Consequently, the manufacturer plans to charge its distributors $10.38 (3 × $3.36) for each unit of product A they purchase.

To calculate the markup percentage that it will earn on the item, the company applies equation #1, as follows:

$$\text{Markup percentage on cost} = \frac{\text{Markup (in dollars and cents)}}{\text{Cost}} \times 100\%$$

$$= \frac{\$6.92}{\$3.46} \times 100\%$$

$$= 200\%$$

Few manufacturers set prices by tripling their product costs. The markup percentage needed or wanted by a firm may, of course, be higher or lower than 200 percent. You can work up the dollars-and-cents value of any markup percentage by using a modification of the markup percentage-on-cost equation.

For example, consider this situation: A manufacturing company seeks a markup of 170 percent on an article that cost $13.50 to produce. To determine just how much this markup would give them in dollars-and-cents figures, the firm works out the following equation:

Markup in dollars and cents   =   Markup percentage × Cost
  =   1.7 × $13.50
  = $22.95

Then, using the basic markup formula, the company sets its selling price:

P   =   C + MU
  = $13.50 + $22.95
  = $36.45

Markups in Retailing

Many retail firms manage and control their inventories by retail prices, rather than by the cost of goods. To arrive at retail selling prices, they use equation #2 above.

An Illustration: A gift-and-novelty chain purchases plush toys from a distributor at a cost per unit of $8.30. Company policy dictates that the selling price of any article of merchandise offered for resale is to be set at twice the cost of the item. (*Keystoning*, or setting the price at double the cost of a product, is a simple and quite common approach in the retailing world.) Thus, an approximate selling price of $16.60 per piece is established for these toys.

The markup percentage is calculated in this manner:

$$\text{Markup percentage on selling price} = \frac{\text{Markup (in dollars and cents)}}{\text{Selling price}} \times 100\%$$

$$= \frac{\$8.30}{\$16.60} \times 100\%$$

$$= 50\%$$

Note: Since $16.60 would make for a rather unusual selling price, the chain will most likely price the toys at $16.50, $16.95, or $17.00.

—Tip 112—

Calculate the size of the initial markup to place on incoming goods.

When planning merchandise requirements for a season or for the year, retailers work at developing an initial markup to place on all incoming goods. This markup is designed to cover the sales, profit, and retail reductions projected for the period. They can determine the initial markup percentage they need by solving this equation:

$$\text{Initial markup percentage} = \frac{\text{Expenses + Retail reductions + Profit}}{\text{Net sales + Retail reductions}}$$

Because they lower the value of the merchandise inventory, the retail reductions listed below must be taken into account during this forward planning:

- Markdowns
- Stock shortages
- Employee discounts
- Customer discounts

An Illustration: The buyer for a sporting goods superstore wants to determine the initial markup needed for the fall-winter season, given the following planned percentages:

Net sales	-	100%
Expenses	-	38%
Profit	-	7%
Stock shortages	-	4%

Employee discounts   -   1%
Customer discounts   -   1%
Markdowns   -   3%

The buyer proceeds to solve the equation:

$$\text{Initial markup percentage} = \frac{\text{Expenses} + \text{Retail reductions} + \text{Profit}}{\text{Net sales} + \text{Retail reductions}}$$

$$= \frac{38\% + 9\% + 7\%}{100\% + 9\%}$$

$$= \frac{54\%}{109\%}$$

$$= 49.5\%$$

The buyer decides to assign an initial markup of 49.5 percent.

—Tip 113—

Learn how to determine maintained markup percentages.

The planned initial markup that the retailer places on incoming goods in advance of a season only approximates the markup that will be realized by the end of the season. Other influences, such as alteration or workroom costs, retail reductions, and cash discounts earned for paying bills early will modify the final, or maintained markup.

The maintained markup is defined in the following formula:

Maintained markup = Net sales − Gross cost of goods sold

Assuming net sales of $2,000,000 and a gross cost of goods of $940,000, the maintained markup in dollars will come to $1,060,000. Or, in percentage terms:

$$\text{Maintained markup percentage} = \frac{\text{Markup dollars}}{\text{Net sales}} \times 100\%$$

$$= \frac{\$1,060,000}{\$2,000,000}$$

$$= 53\%$$

—Tip 114—

Knowing how to calculate average markups can be helpful.

Frequently, retailers seek to calculate the *average markup* they'll be getting for a particular product, price line, classification of goods, merchandise line, or department.

In the illustration below, a buyer who purchases a product from three different suppliers at three different costs tries to determine her average markup.

An Illustration: A buyer orders women's blouses that she retails at $35 each from three different suppliers. To find out what kind of markup the store will average on these goods, she first prepares this table:

	Units	Cost	Priced at Retail	Markup Dollars
Now in stock:	64	$1,056	$2,240	$1,184
Expected in from:				
Supplier #1	60	1,095	2,100	1,005
Supplier #2	48	720	1,680	960
Supplier #3	48	708	1,680	972
Totals:	220	$3,579	$7,700	$4,121

She then enters the appropriate figures into the equation shown below and proceeds to solve the problem:

$$\text{Average markup percentage} = \frac{\text{Total markup dollars}}{\text{Total retail value}} \times 100\%$$

$$= \frac{\$4,121}{\$7,700} \times 100\%$$

$$= 53.5\%$$

APPLYING MARKDOWNS AND DISCOUNTS

A markdown is a reduction in the selling price of a product or service. Retailers are often compelled to take markdowns on merchandise for such reasons as:

- Inept forecasting

- Poor stockkeeping practices

- Buyer errors

- Improper handling of goods by shoppers

- Fashion changes

- Bad weather

- Overstocked conditions

—Tip 115—

Take markdowns when you need to—and take them early!

Don't postpone taking markdowns when they're necessary. The earlier you can dispose of slow-selling, outmoded, damaged, or overstocked merchandise, the better off you'll be. Once they're gone, you can replace them with other goods that you can sell at their regular retail prices.

Shoppers and retailers differ in their perceptions of goods offered at marked-down prices. The shopper who pays $40 for an article of merchandise that sold previously at $60 feels that the transaction resulted in a savings of 33-1/3 percent off the regular selling price. The company that follows the retail method of inventory valuation looks differently at this situation; to keep its bookkeeping on course, the firm calculates its markdown percentage based on the new, marked-down price instead of on the original selling price. Here's how it's done:

$$\text{Markdown percentage} = \frac{\text{Dollar amount of markdown}}{\text{Marked-down selling price}} \times 100\%$$

$$= \frac{\$10}{\$20} \times 100\%$$

$$= 50\%$$

Discounts

Discounts, too, are reductions from the selling prices of products and services. Here are the types of discounts we see in the business sector:

- *Cash discounts* (to encourage the early payment of invoices)

■ *Customer discounts* (granted to certain classes of customers)

■ *Employee discounts*

■ *Introductory discounts* (to introduce a new product or service)

■ *Quantity discounts* (granted on large purchases)

■ *Seasonal discounts* (offered in advance of an upcoming season)

■ *Trade discounts* (to compensate members of the marketing channels of distribution for the parts they play in forwarding goods and services to final users)

Trade Discounts: An Illustration: A manufacturer of small appliances produces an electric iron that generally retails at $27.50 per unit. The appliances, attractively boxed, are packed in cartons of one dozen.

Here is how the manufacturer arranges the various selling prices for the trade:

Retailer's selling price (per dozen)	=	$330.00
Retailer earns gross margin of 44%	=	145.20
Retailer pays wholesaler	=	$184.80
Wholesaler earns gross margin of 15%	=	27.72
Wholesaler pays manufacturer	=	$157.08

Often, a manufacturer signs a contract with a selling agent who is charged with securing orders directly from wholesalers. The agent receives a commission on all sales. Assuming that the small-appliance manufacturing company mentioned above is represented by a selling agent who is to earn a 5-percent commission on sales, the agent will receive $7.85 per dozen and the firm will retain $149.23 per dozen.

SALES-BOOSTING PROMOTIONAL PRICING AIDS

Don't overlook the sales-stimulating effects of certain promotional pricing techniques. Review the list of pricing terms in figure 6-2 and pay particular attention to leader pricing, multi-unit pricing, and price lining.

—Tip 116—

Perk up sales during slower periods with leader price promotions.

Schedule leader price promotions periodically throughout the year. These promotions are perfect when business normally is quiet. For best results, choose well-known items in continuous demand and offer them at reduced prices that the public will immediately recognize as representing excellent buys.

USEFUL REFERENCES

Hirshleifer, Jack and M. Sproul. *Price Theory and Applications*, 4th ed. Englewood Cliffs, N.J.: Prentice-Hall, 1988.

Kotler, Philip and Paul N. Bloom, *Marketing Professional Services*. Englewood Cliffs, N.J.: Prentice-Hall, 1984.

Marshall, A. *More Profitable Pricing*. New York: McGraw-Hill, 1980.

Monroe, Kent B. *Pricing: Making Profitable Decisions*. New York: McGraw-Hill, 1979.

Montgomery, Stephen L. *Profitable Pricing Strategies*. New York: McGraw-Hill, 1988.

Nagle, Thomas T. *The Strategy and Tactics of Pricing: A Guide to Profitable Decision Making*. Englewood Cliffs, N.J.: Prentice-Hall, 1987.

Oxenfeldt, Alfred R. *Pricing Strategies*. New York: AMACOM, 1982.

Symonds, Curtis W. *Pricing for Profit*. New York: AMACOM, 1982.

7/   ENHANCE YOUR FIRM'S ADVERTISING

At the very beginning of chapter 5, you met the "Four P's" of the marketing mix: product, price, promotion, and place. Promotion is itself a mix of three major elements: advertising, personal selling, and sales promotion.

This chapter centers on that first element; the next two chapters target the other components of the promotion mix.

Among other activities, effective management of the advertising function in your business calls for:

- Establishing an advertising budget

- Selecting your target market(s)

- Determining the objective(s) you want to accomplish

- Devising a strategy for reaching your objective(s)

- Choosing suitable media for conveying your message(s) to your target market(s)

- Creating advertisements that will communicate your message(s) clearly and effectively

- Timing your ads strategically

- Evaluating the results of your advertising

PROBLEM INDICATORS IN THE ADVERTISING AREA

Complaints such as those listed below call for your prompt attention:

- Failing to attain planned objectives

- Excessive advertising expenditures

- Disappointing sales response from media advertising

- Poor choice of media

- Too much waste circulation

- Inadequate reach

- Faulty timing of advertisements

- Insufficient number of leads or sales generated by direct mail campaigns

- Instances of poor recall or recognition among targeted customers or prospects

- Friction between the firm and its advertising agency

Target areas for investigation can be seen in figure 7-1.

HOW TO DEVISE A MORE EFFECTIVE PROMOTION MIX

Yes, you can make your promotional dollars work harder and smarter! You can accomplish this by blending the elements of your promotion mix in those proportions that are best suited to your marketing objectives.

—Tip 117—

Review and improve your present promotion mix.

Determine which of the three components of your promotion mix is the most essential to your operation: personal selling, advertising, or sales promotion. Whichever one you select, you'll then need to decide what portion of your overall promotion budget to allocate to that area. Should it be 33-1/3, 50, or 75 percent of total promotion dollars, or somewhere in between? Determine, too, the relative importance of the other two elements and the percentage of budget you should consign to each.

See figure 7-2 for hypothetical promotion mixes for four different business types.

—Tip 118—

Complete next year's advertising budget by Labor Day.

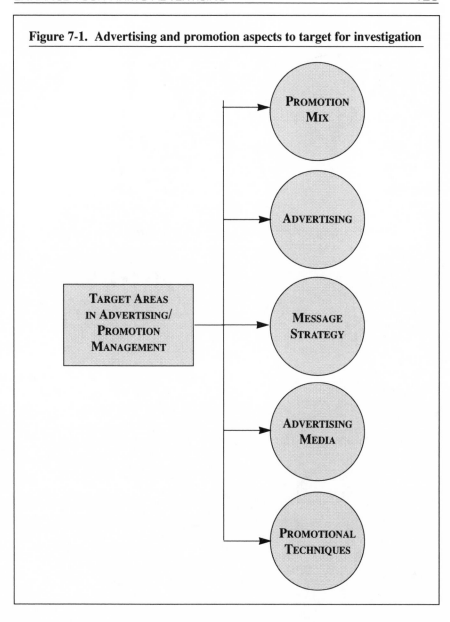

Figure 7-1. Advertising and promotion aspects to target for investigation

To meet the Labor Day deadline, you'll have to nail down your overall promotion budget long before August rolls around. Decide how much to spend next year for promotion, then begin work on your advertising budget.

To learn what percentage of their annual sales volume companies like yours typically allocate to promotion, check with your trade association, Dun &

Figure 7-2. Sample promotion mixes

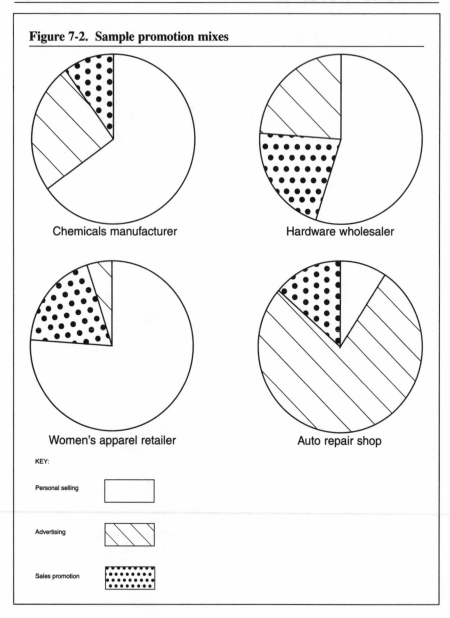

Chemicals manufacturer

Hardware wholesaler

Women's apparel retailer

Auto repair shop

KEY:

Personal selling

Advertising

Sales promotion

Bradstreet, or other commercial sources. Bear in mind, though, that if your business is relatively new, you'll need to spend perhaps twice as much on promotion for the first few years than similar, well-established enterprises.

SECRETS OF SUPERIOR ADVERTISING

You'll get better results from your advertising efforts if you:

■ Create ads that get attention, arouse interest, create desire, and get action

■ Choose the best and most cost-effective media through which to communicate with your target prospects

■ Plan effective campaigns

■ Time your campaigns sensibly

—Tip 119—

Specify your objective(s) for each ad campaign.

Base each advertising campaign on specific goals that you hope to attain. Note that all forms of promotion involve communication; they're designed to inform, persuade, or remind prospects and/or customers. For each campaign, you'll need to determine the kinds of advertising that would best suit your purpose:

■ **Pioneering advertising.** Used to introduce new products, brands, services, promotions, company branches, and so on

■ **Promotional advertising.** Used to sell products and services

■ **Reminder advertising.** Used to reinforce promotional effort and to keep the product, brand, or service alive in the target market's collective mind

■ **Institutional advertising.** Used to promote and popularize a company, institution, or industry

See figure 7-3 for a list of popular promotional objectives.

—Tip 120—

Embellish your print advertising with selected halftones or illustrations.

Figure 7-3. Some promotional objectives

- To announce new products and/or services
- To assist the salesforce
- To attract new buyers
- To build goodwill
- To clear out overstocked or end-of-season goods
- To counter competitive advertising
- To create demand
- To cultivate company/store loyalty
- To differentiate your firm from other companies of the same type
- To encourage repeat business
- To enhance the company's image
- To extend the firm's trading area
- To generate in-store traffic
- To help intermediaries market their offerings
- To increase sales
- To induce passersby to enter the store
- To inform prospective buyers about upcoming promotions
- To introduce a new product, product line, fashion, or service
- To invite consumers or organizations to try a new product or service
- To obtain inquiries
- To open up new territories
- To persuade organizations or consumers to buy
- To promote repeat business
- To publicize the opening of a new plant, branch, or outlet
- To reactivate lost accounts
- To sell goods or services
- To stimulate new business
- To strengthen company-community ties
- To target a new market

All-copy ads are BORING! In every print ad you create, display a halftone (photograph) or an illustration (line or wash drawing), whether it's intended for reproduction in a newspaper or magazine; in a circular, brochure, or catalog; or on a poster or billboard. Design the ad so that the artwork attracts the attention of readers and lures them into the ad copy.

—Tip 121—

Build attention-getters into your print advertising.

Newspapers and magazines are filled with news items, articles, stories, features, and, of course, advertisements. All this clutter is bound to interfere with their readers getting any messages you may place in them. Give your own advertising the chance to be seen; use all the tricks at your command to call attention to it.

Actions to Consider:

■ Leave ample white space around the ad or enclose it within an attractive border.

■ Facilitate reader recognition by using the same typeface and logo in all newspaper and magazine ads.

■ For occasional contrast, present your message in white letters against a dark background (black or a strong color).

■ For car card, poster, and billboard advertisements, provide bright backgrounds that can be seen easily from a distance. (Yellow, orange, and red are excellent choices. So are fluorescent colors.)

■ Enliven billboards by adding animation.

■ Include catchy headlines in your direct mail sales letters and add an ample number of subheads in a second color.

TIPS ON STRENGTHENING MESSAGE STRATEGY

In planning an appropriate strategy for reaching your target market(s), you'll need to:

■ Specify your advertising objective(s)

■ Base your strategy on those objective(s)

■ Decide what to tell your target audience

- Structure your proposition to attract attention and arouse interest

- Write creative, compelling copy that builds in strong appeals (both logical and emotional)

—Tip 122—

Improve your copywriting skills.

Yes, you can become a competent copysmith! Keep the reader firmly in mind whenever you prepare copy for your print advertising. Follow the AIDA Principle: get the reader's *A*ttention, spark *I*nterest in what you're trying to say, kindle the reader's *D*esire to act, and ask for *A*ction in the form of a purchase (or inquiry).

Enhance your advertising copy by following the suggestions offered in the next section.

Actions to Consider:

- Write as though you're talking directly to your target customer or prospect.

- Use the kinds of words and sentences you would ordinarily use in everyday conversation.

- Avoid the passive tense.

- Quickly snare the reader's attention.

- Get the reader involved.

- Build in appeals to rational motives.

- Seek to involve the reader's emotions.

- Emphasize the major features of the product or service.

- Demonstrate the desirability of ownership; show how the buyer will benefit.

- Strive for believability.

- Write persuasively.

- Include one or more testimonials.

- Offer a guarantee.

- Show the reader how to respond to your message.

■ Polish and repolish your copy until you're certain that every word of it makes a contribution toward the whole.

—Tip 123—

Learn how to write headlines that practically leap off the page.

An effective headline will stop readers in their tracks and direct their eyes to the advertising copy. Because one headline can garner far more attention than another, be sure to get plenty of practice writing, revising, rewriting, and polishing provocative headlines that compel reader attention. Create headlines not only for your newspaper and magazine ads but also for your sales letters, brochures, self-mailers, catalogs, and other direct mail pieces. Practice writing how-to, news, question, benefit, and other types of headlines. Become adept at it.

Work just as hard on subheads, too; they enhance and add interest to your copy.

GETTING THE MOST FOR YOUR ADVERTISING DOLLAR

Choosing the right vehicles for transmitting your messages to your target market(s) is a complex undertaking. As you work at media selection, you'll need to take many aspects of the problem into account, for example:

■ **Impact**. The effect of an advertising medium on its readership or audience

■ **Reach**. The number of people (readers, listeners, viewers), households, companies, or other types of organizations who will be exposed to your message(s)

■ **Frequency**. The number of times you expose your targets to your message(s)

■ **Waste Circulation**. Those within the reach of a particular medium who aren't part of your target market

■ **Costs**. Production costs, space costs, and the cost of air time or print advertising.

The Advertising Media

Advertisers send messages to their targets through:

- The print media (newspapers, magazines)

- The air media (radio, TV)

- Direct mail

- The position media (billboards, car cards, posters)

- Other media (telephone books, trade directories, matchbooks, skywriting, and so on)

Figure 7-4 offers a summary of the pros and cons for advertisers of the different media.

—Tip 124—

Choose your print media carefully and look for the better buys.

Newspapers

Low cost and quick response are among the attractions of this medium for advertisers. Over 1,100 newspapers serve the public; these include dailies, weeklies, shoppers' guides, and other types. Most of the advertisers in these publications are retailers or service companies.

Newspapers sell space by the column inch or the agate line; (There are fourteen agate lines to one column inch.) National advertisers pay the highest rates; area retailers and service firms are charged local rates, which are considerably lower. Reduced-rate bulk contracts are available to advertisers who plan to use sizable amounts of space over time.

Comparing Rates: Occasionally, a firm may need to decide which of two (or more) newspapers would represent the best media buy. In such cases, the company may compare the publications' milline rates.* The formula used for the calculations is:

$$\text{Milline Rate} = \frac{\text{Agate Line Rate} \times 1,000,000}{\text{Total Circulation}}$$

For demonstration purposes, consider this information submitted by two newspapers vying for the same retailer's advertising.

---

*The milline rate provides the cost per million readers for a newspaper ad.

Newspaper	Line Rate	Circulation
no. 1	$3.85	264,000
no. 2	2.70	171,000

To ascertain which newspaper offers the better buy, we calculate milline rates for both:

$$\text{Milline Rate, no. 1} = \frac{\$3,850,000}{264,000} = \$14.58$$

$$\text{Milline Rate, no. 2} = \frac{\$2,700,000}{171,000} = \$15.79$$

Obviously, the retailer would save some money by placing the advertisement in newspaper no. 1.

However, the milline rate formula has one drawback: the fraction's denominator shows the newspaper's *total* circulation; this figure may include many suburban and out-of-town readers who normally don't shop locally. Thus, there may be considerable waste circulation.

A better, more discriminating formula is available for comparing newspaper buys: the truline rate. It differs from the milline rate in that the fraction's denominator is limited to the circulation *in the retailer's trading area:*

This is the formula:

$$\text{Truline Rate} = \frac{\text{Agate Line Rate} \times 1,000,000}{\text{Circulation in Trading Area}}$$

For the sake of illustration, let's assume that the retailer in question researched the problem further and obtained the following data from the two newspapers:

Newspaper	Line Rate	Circulation in Trading Area
#1	$3.85	207,000
#2	2.70	164,000

Note the effect of using truline, rather than milline, rates to compare publications:

$$\text{Truline Rate, no. 1} = \frac{\$3,850,000}{207,000} = \$18.60$$

$$\text{Truline Rate, no. 2} = \frac{\$2,700,000}{164,000} = \$14.58$$

As we can see, newspaper no. 2 would be a much better buy for the retailer.

Figure 7-4. The mass media: Advantages and disadvantages for advertisers

Newspapers

Advantages:
Short lead time
Real flexibility
Cost per 1,000 readers: Low to moderate
Quick response
Good coverage of market
Readers can clip out ads, coupons

Disadvantages:
Brief ad life
Short exposure
Some secondary readership
Much waste circulation
Clutter (competition from other ads and news items)
Poor reproduction of photographs

Magazines

Advantages:
A long ad life may attract responses for many months
Substantial amount of secondary readership
High market selectivity (demographic, geographic)
Reader loyalty
Source credibility
Prestigious environment for advertising
Good reproduction of photographs
Availability of color

Disadvantages:
Lengthy lead time
No flexibility
Waste circulation
Cost per 1,000 readers: Moderate

Radio

Advantages:
Ultra-short lead time
Extreme flexibility
Cost per 1,000 listeners: Low
Rapid response
Good market selectivity
Audience loyalty

Disadvantages:
Ultra-brief ad life
Limited communication vehicle; appeals to only one sense
Limited audience attention
Message lost after transmission
Audience fragmentation (many stations to choose from)

Figure 7-4. Continued

Television

Advantages:
Some flexibility
Extensive reach
High impact
Quick response
Versatility (involves the sense of sight as well as hearing)
Moderate-to-high viewer attention

Disadvantages:
Short message life
High cost of air time
High cost of producing commercials
Considerable clutter
Cost per 1,000 viewers: Low to moderate
Little selectivity

Direct Mail

Advantages:
High selectivity (can pinpoint specific groups)
Flexibility
High persuasibility
Little or no clutter
Results can be tracked

Disadvantages:
Cost per 1,000 recipients: Moderate to high
Substantial lead time
Considered junk mail by many recipients

Outdoor and Transit

Advantages:
Captive readership
Some flexibility
Repeat exposure
Low cost per 1,000 readers
Little or no clutter

Disadvantages:
Little or no selectivity
Limited message length

Magazines

Among other benefits, magazines offer high market selectivity and long ad life. Most advertisers in these publications are manufacturers or producers; financial or other service institutions (banks, insurance companies, and so on); or large-scale retailers.

Most magazines can be classified as general consumer, news, business, financial, trade, professional, or farm publications. A tremendous number of special interest magazines are also available.

Choosing magazine(s) in which to place your advertising calls for calculating and comparing rates, much like the milline and truline comparisons between newspapers that we've already seen. To select the best buy(s), use the following equation:

$$\text{Cost per } 1,000 \text{ readers} = \frac{\text{Page rate} \times 1,000}{\text{Circulation}}$$

Let's compare the cost per 1,000 readers for three different magazines, all reaching the kinds of readers you're interested in:

Magazine	Page Cost	Circulation
#1	$ 9,870	353,500
#2	11,760	504,800
#3	7,445	237,100

We determine the cost per 1,000 readers for each publication as shown below:

$$\text{Cost per } 1,000 \text{ readers, no. } 1 = \frac{\$9,870,000}{353,500} = \$27.92$$

$$\text{Cost per } 1,000 \text{ readers, no. } 2 = \frac{\$11,760,000}{504,800} = \$23.29$$

$$\text{Cost per } 1,000 \text{ readers, no. } 3 = \frac{\$7,445,000}{237,100} = \$31.40$$

Now, the best buy is clearly magazine no. 2.

Note that magazine space for a full-page ad will cost you less than the space you may need for two 1/2-page or four 1/4-page ads. You'll pay proportionately more for fractional page space, often 10 percent to 20 percent more. To determine your cost per 1,000 readers for ads under one page in size, use this variation of the basic equation:

$$\text{Cost per } 1,000 \text{ readers} = \frac{\text{Ad cost} \times 1,000}{\text{Circulation}}$$

Incidentally, you can use the same approach when comparing costs across media lines; it's useful for newspapers, magazines, radio, TV, position and supplemental media, and even direct mail distributions. When considering different media types, the second half of the equation remains as it is, but you'll need to amend the first half so that it reads: "Cost per 1,000 readers, listeners, viewers, or recipients (of direct mail literature)."

—Tip 125—

Look for good buys in air time.

Radio

Low cost, quick response, and audience loyalty are among radio's attractions for advertisers. Stay away from morning (and evening) drive time as well as the other daytime hours; rates for those "dayparts" are the highest. Concentrate on the off-peak hours: nights, post-midnight, and weekends are the least expensive. Or, arrange for a run-of-station schedule.

Television

TV can exert a tremendous impact on its audience. However, broadcast time can be costly, especially on the big networks. Spots on local TV, though, are not all that expensive. You'll pay the lowest rates between midnight and 6 A.M.

Use the equation below to compare the costs of air time between two or more broadcast stations (radio, TV, or both):

$$\text{Cost per } 1,000 \text{ households} = \frac{\text{Cost of air time} \times 1,000}{\text{Number of households reached}}$$

Note that the equation doesn't take into account the cost of producing the commercial, which in the case of TV can be considerable.

—Tip 126—

Include direct mail in your advertising plans.

Direct mail is a powerful and amazingly selective medium that enables advertisers to forward their messages directly to their target market(s). It can be used profitably by almost every company, regardless of its type.

You'll find more information about direct mail later in this chapter under Tip 130.

—Tip 127—

Weigh the merits of the position media for your advertising.

The position media (posters, bus and subway car cards, and billboards) may offer opportunities for some companies to inform the public about their places of business or to advertise their brands, goods, or services. Captive audiences and a low cost per 1,000 readers are the major attractions.

—Tip 128—

Grab most offers of cooperative advertising.

Occasionally, a manufacturer will encourage its distributors to promote its products by offering to pay half of the cost of media advertising. Or, two or more retailers or service companies will plan a joint promotion and agree to share the attendant expenses. If and when these exciting invitations come your way, accept them graciously; chances are that you'll benefit considerably from most of these mutual promotions.

—Tip 129—

Look for opportunities to barter your goods and/or services.

You may be able to strike an occasional deal with a radio or TV station by offering to exchange your excess products and/or services for broadcast time. Or, perhaps, by providing a combination of goods and some cash. The stations may give away your goods in connection with a contest or other type of promotion or award them as prizes on quiz shows.

Similarly, magazine publishers may be amenable to a proposition from you about bartering for remnant space. There are also barter agencies through which, for a fee, you can exchange your goods and/or services for those of other companies.

INCREASE SALES WITH THESE THREE PROMOTIONAL POWERHOUSES

Traditionally, most companies allocate the bulk of their advertising funds to the print and/or air media and pay little attention to three other avenues of promotion that may offer extraordinary sales potential. You owe it to yourself to explore:

- Direct mail marketing
- Telemarketing
- Marketing via the information superhighway

—Tip 130—

Put more time, effort, and money into direct mail.

Many billions of dollars are spent each year on direct mail. Manufacturers and wholesalers use direct mail to get orders and obtain leads. Retailers use it to bring traffic into their stores, sign up charge customers, and sell merchandise directly to consumers. Service companies rely on it to publicize and sell their services.

Explore ways to make better use of direct mail in your company.

Actions to Consider:

- Read up on—or take a course in—direct marketing.
- Review your operation to find out those areas where you can apply and benefit from direct mail promotions.
- Become familiar with the elements of the standard direct mail package (sales letter, order form, cover envelope, and return envelope).
- Look into the wide range of formats available to direct mailers, from broadsides, brochures, and package stuffers to self-mailers and catalogs.

- Find out about the many techniques and gadgets that can be used to call attention to your direct mail.

- Subscribe to *Direct Marketing*, the top publication in its field.*

- Ask the media about accepting advertising on a per inquiry or per order basis.

- Compile mailing lists from such sources as industrial and trade directories, business-to-business telephone books, membership lists of fraternal and other organizations, and so on.

- Request catalogs from list compilers and brokers, and rent lists from them.

- Learn how to maintain and update your mailing lists.

- Strengthen your direct mail propositions by including testimonials.

- Increase returns by guaranteeing buyers their money back if they aren't completely satisfied.

- Set up a failsafe procedure for tracking your mailings and recording the results.

- Put in an 800 line and advertise the toll-free number in your direct mail literature.

- Prepare and distribute a catalog of your offerings.

- Include an occasional promotion in your direct mail: a special sale, coupons, a premium offer, and so on.

- Look into cooperative mailings.

—Tip 131—

Initiate a telemarketing program.

If you haven't already researched this avenue of promotion, contact an outside telemarketing agency to find out what it can do for you. Or, better still, read a few books on the subject and then launch a program of your own.** (For additional information, see the section on "Effective Strategies for Selling by Phone" in the next chapter.)

---

*Address: 224 Seventh Avenue, Garden City, NY 11530. The telephone number is: (516) 746-6700.

**For further reading on telemarketing, see the bibliography at the end of chapter 8.

—Tip 132—

Hop onto the information superhighway.

Reportedly, some 25 million people around the globe now use their computers to tap into the Internet—and their numbers are still growing! They cruise through cyberspace seeking all kinds of information of interest to them. This enormous, grass-roots communication network bears enormous potential for enterprises of all types.

Today's personal computers not only process and print information but also transmit and receive faxes within seconds, accept and record telephone calls, speed E-mail to countless destinations, put catalogs on line, take and fulfill orders, and reply to inquiries from other computers.

A powerful tool, the personal computer is especially valuable for business-to-business marketing. By using the tools of your desk top computer, you can obtain sales leads, locate and reach dealers and vendors, promote products or services, build a company or brand image, attract new customers, and accomplish a host of other profitable feats.

USEFUL REFERENCES

Bacon, Mark S. *Do-It-Yourself Direct Marketing: Secrets for Small Business.* New York: Wiley, 1994.

Book, Albert C. and Dennis Schick. *Fundamentals of Copy and Layout.* Lincolnwood, Ill.: NTC, 1990.

Book, Albert C. et al. *The Radio and Television Commercial*, 2d ed. Lincolnwood, Ill.: NTC, 1986.

Bovee, Courtland and William F. Arens. *Contemporary Advertising*, 5th ed. Homewood, Ill.: Irwin, 1993.

Burstiner, Irving. *Mail Order Selling: How to Market Almost Anything by Mail*, 3rd ed. New York: Wiley, 1995.

Caples, John. *Tested Advertising Methods*, 4th ed. Englewood Cliffs, N.J.: Prentice-Hall, 1986.

David, Bruce E. *The Profitable Advertising Manual: A Handbook for Small Business*, 2d ed. Twinsburg, Ohio: Worthprinting, 1986.

Demoney, Jerry and Susan E. Meyer. *Pasteups and Mechanicals: A Step-by-Step Guide to Preparing Art for Reproduction*. New York: Watson-Guptill, 1982.

Duffy, Ben. *Advertising Media and Markets*. New York: Garland, 1985.

Harper, C. R. *Mailing List Strategies: A Guide to Direct Mail Success*. New York: McGraw-Hill, 1986.

Klein, Erica Levy. *Write Great Ads: A Step-by-Step Approach*. New York: Wiley, 1990.

Kremer, John. *The Complete Mail-Order Sourcebook*. New York: Wiley, 1992.

Levine, Mindy N. and Susan Frank. *In Print: A Concise Guide to Graphic Arts and Printing for Small Business and Nonprofit Organizations*. Englewood Cliffs, N.J.: Prentice-Hall, 1984.

Maas, Jane. *Better Brochures, Catalogs and Mailing Pieces*. New York: St. Martin's Press, 1984.

Pickens, Judy E. *The Copy-to-Press Handbook: Preparing Words and Art for Print*. New York: Wiley, 1985.

Russell, J. and G. Verrill. *Otto Kleppner's Advertising Procedure*, 9th ed. Englewood Cliffs, N.J.: Prentice-Hall, 1986.

Stone, Bob. *Successful Direct Marketing Methods*, 5th ed. Lincolnwood, Ill.: NTC, 1993.

Woods, Bob and Herbert Holtie. *Printing and Production for Promotional Materials*. New York: Van Nostrand Reinhold, 1986.

8/ REVITALIZE YOUR SELLING ACTIVITIES

Most company managements allocate well over 50 percent of their promotion budgets to personal selling activity. That's because incoming revenue dollars spin the wheels of their money-making machines, maintain the operation's solvency, and generate profits for the owner(s). The need for professionalism in directing the selling end, then, is blatantly evident.

PROBLEM INDICATORS IN THE SALES AREA

Be ready to move quickly if you come across one or more of these disturbing sales-related situations:

- Losing customers
- Failing to attain sales goals
- Inadequate coverage of accounts
- An increase in the average cost of a sales call
- The average order shrinking in size
- Experiencing difficulty in getting reorders
- Closing ratios that continue to drop
- Signs of deteriorating salesforce morale
- A disturbing rate of turnover in the salesforce
- Instances of customer dissatisfaction with salespeople
- Conflicts between salespeople and sales manager
- Inadequately trained salespeople

- Increasing expenditures for travel and entertainment
- Too much time spent by salespeople in office or on paperwork
- Delays in forwarding orders
- Errors on order forms submitted by salespeople
- Mistakes in recording orders received in the mail and/or over the telephone

For areas in which you may be able to effect profitable change, see figure 8-1.

BUILDING A TOP-NOTCH SALES TEAM

Building a salesforce is no easy task. Accomplishing this feat requires thoughtful forward planning, followed by organizing, coordinating, directing, and evaluating all the necessary elements: the finances, personnel, systems, procedures, and work activities.

The process of salesforce formation and management involves:

- Establishing the sales budget
- Determining sales objectives
- Structuring the salesforce
- Setting up a compensation program
- Selecting, hiring, and training salespeople
- Assigning territories
- Motivating the salespeople to do their best
- Reviewing salesperson performance

—Tip 133—

Start by exploring alternatives to your own salesforce.

Before launching your investigation into the sales aspects indicated in figure 8-1, make up your mind as to whether or not you really need a sales contingent of your own. You may be able to avoid the extraordinary outlay of capital associated with hiring, training, and maintaining a salesforce.

Ask these questions of yourself:

Figure 8-1. Personal selling aspects to target for investigation

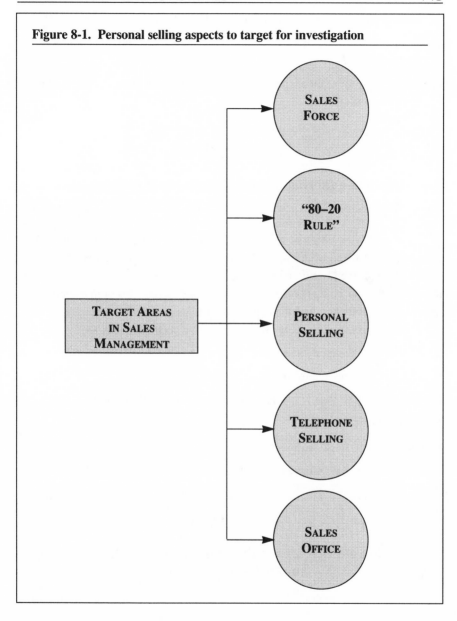

- Could you produce as much revenue through sales offices that you open in two or three major population centers?

- Might you be able to reach a comparable level of sales (or perhaps even a higher level) by contracting with a selling agent to dispose of your entire production?

■ Would a commission broker be a better choice?

■ Would you do as well or even better by taking on several manufacturers' representatives?

■ Can you sell substantial quantities of your products and/or services through direct marketing?

—Tip 134—

Conduct a thorough vertical audit of the sales division.

Delve into the personal selling end. Find out what's going on, what has happened in the past, and what's scheduled for the future. Examine the objectives that were chosen for the sales division. Look into its various departments and sections: the work activities being performed or contemplated; the roles of managers, assistants, and subordinates; and the caliber and performance of the salesforce.

Before you start, though, you need to settle such questions as:

■ What is your company's mission?

■ What are your objectives for the sales area?

■ Who are your target prospects—consumers, organizations, or both?

■ What are these people and/or organizations like?

■ What are their needs and wants?

■ Can you supply their needs and wants?

—Tip 135—

Find out if you have the right kind—and the right number—of salespeople.

Every company attempts to adapt its selling approaches to meet the needs of the prospects it has targeted. This fact applies to salesforce formation as well. You'll need to decide, in accordance with your objectives, whether your sales contingent should consist of order takers or order getters and if you ought to employ any missionary salespeople or technical specialists.

Typically, the more successful salespeople appear to be:

ambitious	honest
bright	persevering
confident	personable
dependable	resourceful
emotionally	self-confident
stable	sincere
enthusiastic	tactful

Hopefully, your sales staff possesses most of the above-mentioned attributes.

Determining Salesforce Size

Traditionally, the number of salespeople required to do the job is calculated by dividing the total workload by that portion of the workload that an average salesperson may be expected to perform. Most often, this computation is made in terms of sales volume, using the following equation:

$$\text{Number of salespeople needed} = \frac{\text{Sales volume forcasted for next year}}{\text{Average volume per salesperson}}$$

Some companies base their approach on the number of accounts currently on their books, as follows:

$$\text{Number of salespeople needed} = \frac{\text{Total number of accounts}}{\text{Average number of accounts per salesperson}}$$

Still other firms rely on an equation that considers the number of sales calls to be made during the year:

$$\text{Number of salespeople needed} = \frac{\text{Total number of planned sales calls}}{\text{Average number of calls per salesperson}}$$

—Tip 136—

Draft and institute new, improved training programs.

Changing circumstances and an environment in constant flux dictate the need for continually updating salesforce training. Together with your sales manager, review your training programs. Determine current needs, design curricula, choose instructional methods, prepare training schedules, and arrange for program evaluation.

Be sure to cover the following topics:

- Company knowledge
- Product knowledge (including pricing)
- Competitor knowledge
- Customer knowledge
- Time management
- Call reports and expense accounts
- Territory management
- Promotional programs
- New-product introductions
- Sales training

—Tip 137—

Question your present compensation approaches.

Examine your current compensation plan(s). You may be able to effect changes that will lead to an increase in sales revenues, produce more profit, and/or gain another point or two in market share.

Actions to Consider:

- Start off sales trainees with a modest but fair weekly salary.
- As soon as they've completed their training, give order takers a substantial raise.
- After training, shift your order getters from a straight salary to a straight commission basis and give them a sensible drawing account. If the situation calls for it, provide them with an expense account with caps on how much can be spent daily for food and lodging.
- Pay missionary salespeople and technical specialists salaries that are competitive with the rest of the industry.
- Take territorial differences into account when setting commission percentages.

■ Offer salespeople a slightly higher commission rate on orders for slow-moving goods.

■ Stimulate the sale of high-margin products by paying more commission on these orders.

■ Add an extra point or two to the salesperson's commission for initial orders from newly opened accounts.

■ Award a congratulatory bonus to all who exceed their sales quotas.

■ Occasionally, build short-term excitement by running a contest or other incentive.

—Tip 138—

Reassure yourself that you've chosen the right sales manager.

Like any other manager, the sales executive performs all four management functions: planning, organizing, directing, and controlling the activities of subordinates. To exercise these functions ably, the sales manager must possess strong communication and leadership skills, an astute understanding of company goals and organization, a facility for diagnosing and solving problems, and, of course, a competent grasp of the dynamics of selling itself.

Among other activities, the sales manager:

■ Recruits salespeople

■ Trains the recruits

■ Monitors their progress

■ Assigns territories

■ Maintains contact with field salespeople by mail and telephone

■ Oversees intermediate and advanced training

■ Builds a strong, positive team spirit among the salespeople

■ Evaluates individual and group performance

■ Watches territorial yields

■ Reviews expense accounts and call reports

■ Prepares sales and expense analyses

■ Keeps selling costs in line

—Tip 139—

Formally evaluate your salespeople at least once a year.

Instruct your sales manager to evaluate all members of the salesforce annually. (*Note:* Semiannual assessments would be even better!) Each appraisal is to be followed by a formal meeting between the sales manager and the salesperson at which the latter's record is reviewed, problems are discussed and solutions proposed, and the two collaborate in setting goals for the coming year.

You'll need to develop a suitable form for rating your salespeople. (See figure 8-2 for suggestions as to the criteria, subjective as well as objective, to build into the evaluation instrument.)

FOLLOW THE 80-20 RULE TO DOUBLE YOUR SALES

In chapter 5, you became acquainted with the 80-20 Rule, a concept with interesting applications to a number of marketing aspects (see the section in that chapter entitled "Consolidate and Improve your Product Line").

Now, you'll see how to impress the 80-20 Rule into service to improve the productivity of your salesforce.

—Tip 140—

Make a practice run: Check the 80-20 Rule with your customer list.

Examine your current customer base. Find out who are your most important customers and how much these top accounts collectively contribute to your sales revenues. List the names of all the accounts on your books, then enter next to each name the total amount of all purchases each customer made over the past twelve months. Rearrange the list in terms of the sales volume each contributed, from the highest to the lowest. More likely than not, you'll discover that one-fifth of your customers accounted for approximately four-fifths of last year's sales.

Figure 8-2. Criteria for evaluating salesperson performance

Useful quantitative measures:

Average order size

Average cost per call

Average cost per sale

Direct selling expenses-to-sales ratio

Number of new accounts opened

Number of orders taken

Number of cancelled orders

Number of sales calls made

Order/call ratio

Percentage deviation from last year's sales

Percentage deviation from sales quota

Ratio of new accounts to established accounts

Total sales volume

Useful qualitative criteria:

Communication skills

Company knowledge

Competitor knowledge

Customer knowledge

Customer relations

Order form accuracy

Personal appearance

Planning and routing of sales calls

Product knowledge

Promptness in submitting reports

Selling expertise

Time management

—Tip 141—

**Now, get ready to boost sales sharply by applying
the 80-20 Rule to your salesforce.**

Check your sales records for the past year. List the names all your sales-people. Next to these names, write down the total sales each person brought in. Reorder the list by these amounts, in descending order. Then, draw a line under the top 20 percent of the names; these people are your top sales producers. Count off the bottom 20 percent and draw a line just above the first name in that group; these are your weakest salespeople. (Note that you may need to temper this judgment somewhat because substantial differences may exist among territorial assignments.)

—Tip 142—

Retrain and remotivate your poor producers.

The lowest 20 percent on your list are your poorest producers. Work with your sales manager in designing a powerful retraining program, one that should quickly bring the productivity of these salespeople up to par. Also, put into place a strong incentive plan. Set a time limit of, say, 45 or 60 days for those individuals who go through the program to demonstrate their progress. Dismiss those who show no improvement.

—Tip 143—

Enlist the expertise of your top performers.

Direct your sales manager to bring in the top three or four salespeople to aid the retraining by demonstrating their selling techniques and coaching the poor producers in closing sales.

—Tip 144—

Motivate the middle 60 percent on your list of salespeople.

Bring into play motivational tools that will both challenge and inspire your salespeople.

Actions to Consider:

■ Build up their self-esteem through positive reinforcement.

■ Show them that their jobs are secure and that the company depends on their contributions.

■ Recognize their accomplishments. Award certificates of merit, bonuses, extra vacation days, or other incentives for outstanding performance.

■ Set up cash incentive programs on daily, weekly, and monthly bases.

■ Offer promotions (to team, district, or regional managers) to those who make the greatest strides.

■ Offer personal growth opportunities (to attend a seminar or workshop, to take college courses, etc.).

PROFESSIONAL SELLING SECRETS

Provide your salespeople with intensive training in the art of selling. Do this by teaching them each step, one at a time, in the personal selling process.

Here are brief descriptions of those steps:

■ **Prospecting**. Searching for likely buyers of your goods and/or services.

■ **Qualifying Prospects and the Preapproach**. Often referred to as "pre-call planning," this is when the salesperson tries to learn as much as possible about the prospects: their needs and wants, their likes and dislikes, whether or not they have the necessary finances to buy whatever is being sold; how best to reach them, and so on. Arranging interviews with the prospects concludes this phase of the selling process.

- **The Approach**. The first minute or two of initial contact between salesperson and prospect. During this ultrabrief phase, the salesperson will try to develop a rapport with the prospect.

- **The Sales Presentation**. That portion of the sales interview during which the salesperson introduces the product or service, presents its major selling points, and outlines the benefits it can bring to the buyer.

- **Meeting and Overcoming Objections**. Often, a prospect will voice one or more objections during the presentation, perhaps to the purchase price quoted, the product's quality or durability, the company that the salesperson represents, or some other perceived problem. Experienced salespeople, already familiar with such objections, will try to resolve each problem as it comes up.

- **The Close**. This step marks the end of the sales presentation. It's brought about by the use of closing techniques that secure the prospect's agreement to buy. The salesperson then gets the customer's signature on the order.

- **The Follow-Up**. After having closed the sale, the salesperson thanks the customer, tells that person that the decision to buy was indeed wise, and promises to check back after the order has been delivered to make sure that the customer is completely satisfied.

The Retail Selling Process

Retail selling differs somewhat from selling in the field. For example, no prospecting is necessary; shoppers are attracted to the store by advertising, publicity, window displays, and other forms of promotion. Another difference between the two types of personal selling is that, after the customer has agreed to buy the merchandise, the sales associate will suggest that he or she purchase an additional, usually related, item. Among retailers, this is known as "suggestion selling."

—Tip 145—

Enhance your salespeople's prospecting skills.

Show your salespeople how and where to find likely buyers. Advise them to search through sales records for old, discontinued accounts and to ask their present accounts for referrals. Suggest that they cold-canvass residences and/or places of business. Teach them to consult such additional sources as:

- Business and trade directories
- Telephone books (consumers; business-to-business)
- Libraries
- Trade associations
- City, county, and state records
- Membership lists of various organizations

Show your salespeople, too, that management is eager to help ease their task of locating prospective buyers. Commit some promotion dollars to securing the names and addresses of potential buyers through media advertising, direct mail, and/or "teleprospecting."

—Tip 146—

Polish their qualifying, preapproach, and approach techniques.

Set up a series of four weekly meetings, each concentrating on one or more of the steps in the selling process. Avoid conflicts with normal sales activity by scheduling the meetings for Friday afternoons or evenings, or Saturday mornings.

At the first meeting, show them how to:

- Qualify the prospects they locate
- Conduct preapproach activities
- Arrange for the sales visit

—Tip 147—

Remodel and energize their sales presentations.

The two most common approaches used by salespeople in the field are: (1) selling by formula, and (2) needs-satisfaction selling (selling by responding to and fulfilling customer needs).

Selling by formula is a product (or service) oriented approach. It entails preparing and then committing to memory a standardized sales presentation suitable for all prospective buyers. Generally, the format follows the AIDA principle (see chapter 7, Tip 122). Included in the presentation are routine coverage of the main selling points of the product/service and rote responses to the more commonly voiced objections.

Needs-satisfaction selling calls for individualized attention by the salesperson, who assumes that each prospect has special needs and concerns. Usually, considerable investigation is required; information needs to be gathered, problems must be discussed, and solutions should be sought.

You'll need to select the better selling approach for your purposes. Typically, selling by formula is the method of choice for goods and/or services that are popular, well-promoted, and less expensive.

At this second session, engage in role playing: Ask one salesperson to act as the prospective buyer and another to try to sell that person. Then, have the entire group critique the presentation. Repeat the procedure several times, each time with a different pair of individuals.

—Tip 148—

Bring in your top three performers to demonstrate how they handle objections and their closing techniques.

For this session, ask your top salespeople to teach the others their approaches to meeting and overcoming the different types of objections that prospects may voice during sales presentations. Then, have them show their various methods of closing sales.

—Tip 149—

Coach your salespeople in an effective follow-up procedure.

The prime objective behind the follow-up is to cement a long-term relationship between customer and salesperson. Plan an effective procedure for this last step in the personal selling process. Then, teach it to your salespeople and give them plenty of practice until it becomes second nature to them.

EFFECTIVE STRATEGIES FOR SELLING BY PHONE

Reputedly, the average cost of a sales visit now runs well over $300. You owe it to yourself to explore the potential of telephone selling; often, this avenue can accomplish much the same result as an in-person presentation—and at far lower cost.

—Tip 150—

Explore the potential business an outside telemarketing service can send your way.

Perhaps you've already been briefed by a telemarketing company about how it can help your business. If you haven't, check the latest issue of *Direct Marketing* for a listing of some of these organizations. Telemarketing firms offer both inbound and outbound telemarketing and experienced staffs. They can tailor a program to your needs that will give you orders (or leads) at a fair price. By using this service, you'll avoid the expense of designing your own program and telemarketing department, installing additional telephone lines and equipment, hiring and training salespeople, developing effective scripts, and so on.

—Tip 151—

Set up and equip a suitable area for your in-house telephone sales operation.

For your telemarketing department, you'll need enough space for several work stations, each provided with an ergonomic chair, desk, and telephone. Soundproof the area as well as you can: Put in an accoustic ceiling, panel the work stations, and lay carpet down on the floors. Provide good lighting throughout, and maintain good ventilation and a comfortable room temperature at all times.

—Tip 152—

Decide on the qualifications your telephone salespeople should have.

For your new operation, seek telemarketers who you believe possess the traits of successful salespeople that were mentioned earlier in this chapter. In addition to those characteristics, each person you hire should have:

- A pleasant speaking voice
- A positive attitude
- A warm, friendly personality
- Good common sense
- Patience
- Powers of persuasion

Moreover, a telephone salesperson should be:

- Able to withstand frustration
- A competent communicator
- A good listener
- Capable of establishing rapport quickly
- Inured against rejection
- Sincere

—Tip 153—

Estimate the number of telephone salespeople you need.

At the outset, hire an experienced telemarketer to manage your new telephone team. Fill that person in on all the details: your company's mission, objectives, history, products and/or services, organization, and so on. After this indoctrination, discuss the type of telephone selling that needs to be done. Ask lots of questions about telemarketing. Most likely, your new team manager will inform you that telemarketing is a numbers game; that one person can make just so many calls per hour; that some prospects won't be in to answer the call; that, of those who do pick up the phone, some will hang up within moments and without comment; that others will listen to part or all of the message and then respond in the negative, and that only a few will be receptive to the offer.

Get your expert's opinion as to how many calls of all types an average telemarketer can handle in one day. Armed with this information, you can calculate how many telephone salespeople you'll need by modifying the familiar workload equation to read:

$$\text{Number of telemarketers needed} = \frac{\text{Planned number of calls per day}}{\text{Average number of daily calls made per telemarketer}}$$

At a later date, you might consider experimenting with automatic dialing equipment and sales presentation tapes. You may find that this approach pays off royally.

—Tip 154—

Devise an effective telesales training program.

Settle on specific objectives before you begin planning your training program. Do you want your telemarketers to obtain leads for your field salespeople? Answer inquiries? Solicit orders directly? Give information to your accounts? Announce new promotions or price changes?

You'll need to teach them how to:

- Get the right person on the phone in the first place
- Hold that individual's attention
- Establish rapport quickly
- Deliver the presentation
- Sense what the prospect is thinking
- Successfully answer all objections

Actions to Consider:

- Make scriptwriting a collaborative exercise between the telemarketing staff and the team manager.
- Try out different scripts; adopt the one(s) that pull best.

- Direct scripts at the target prospect; write with a clear understanding of what this person is like.

- Make the offer attractive, even unique—and make it eminently believable.

- Sell the sizzle; stress buyer benefits rather than product attributes.

- Teach the trainees how to respond to frequently raised objections.

- Show them how to close the sale.

- Check into available telemarketing software.

—Tip 155—

Compare each salesperson's performance to total team production.

Prepare a record card for each telephone salesperson. Keep track of all production details on a per-hour basis; this makes it easy to evaluate and compare the contributions of part-timers as well as full-time personnel. Each week, tally all information on the record cards in order to compute "batting averages" for the entire department. Then, compare each telemarketer's production to total team production.

Record and compare such data as the:

- Average number of calls dialed per hour (total number of calls dialed during the week, divided by the number of hours worked)

- Average number of unanswered calls per hour (not-in, to be called again)

- Average number of presentations completed per hour

- Average number of sales consummated per hour

- Average sales volume produced per hour

If you've targeted the consumer market, you'll discover that weekends are especially fruitful. During the week, call between 9 A.M. and 5 P.M.—and evenings from 7 P.M. to 9 P.M. Your chances of talking to business buyers are, of course, much better. Call organizations on weekdays during regular office hours.

—Tip 156—

Build on success: Expand your in-house telemarketing operation.

Yes, telemarketing is definitely a numbers game. If you now employ four telemarketers who collectively consummate 300 sales in an average week, adding another two to your staff should boost your weekly take to around 450 sales. That is, of course, if they've been well-trained and have accumulated a few weeks of experience.

HOW TO ENHANCE
SALES-OFFICE EFFICIENCY

A well-managed sales office is a vital adjunct to any salesforce. The office staff maintains a close liaison with the field salespeople; accepts, checks, and processes orders; answers inquiries responsibly; and handles complaints sensibly. The higher you can raise the efficiency of your sales office, the smoother it will run and the greater will be the volume brought in by your sales representatives— and by the office as well.

—Tip 157—

Audit your sales office.

One by one, probe the following aspects of the office to identify, and formulate solutions to, any problems you spot:

- Work activity
- The staff
- Office layout, furniture, and furnishings
- Equipment, systems, and procedures

Actions to Consider:

- Keep the staff informed about products, prices, terms, special promotions, and other operational details so that they can respond intelligently to questions from customers.

- Through short-term job assignments, rotate all personnel so that they may be able to, in emergencies, fulfill the duties and responsibilities of any and all positions in the department.

■ Determine if any changes can be made in the layout that will permit work activity to flow more smoothly.

■ Analyze the daily workload. See to it that it's spread out evenly, that no one person is overburdened, and that all tasks are continually prioritized.

■ Experiment with rearranging (or even replacing) some of the furniture, furnishings, and equipment so as to create a more pleasant atmosphere.

■ Review all service contracts for machines and equipment. Decide which contracts shouldn't be renewed and if replacing any equipment might be a better choice. Consider upgrading, rather than replacing, older computers.

■ Improve your order-handling system. Record each order as it arrives, whether it comes in by mail or over the telephone, or is brought in by a salesperson. Check the order carefully, then route it to the credit section for approval and subsequent forwarding to bookkeeping and shipping.

■ Explore the benefits to be gained by installing a voice-mail system.

—Tip 158—

**Make sure you've placed a seasoned executive
in the office manager's position.**

For the office manager's job, you need an able administrator who:

■ Is familiar with all aspects of the work

■ Can prioritize readily

■ Knows how to schedule and apportion the work

■ Demonstrates excellent interpersonal relations

■ Has a good working knowledge of office machines and equipment

■ Succeeds in maintaining a high level of morale

USEFUL REFERENCES

Alexander, Roy. *Secrets of Closing Sales.* Englewood Cliffs, N.J.: Prentice-Hall, 1989.

Bencin, Richard L. *Strategic Telemarketing.* Philadelphia: Swansea Press, 1987.

Burstiner, Irving. *Basic Retailing*, 2d ed. Homewood, Ill.: Irwin, 1991.

————. *Mail Order Selling*, 3rd ed. New York: Wiley, 1995.

Churchill, Gilbert A. et al. *Sales Force Management*, 4th ed. Homewood, Ill.: Irwin, 1992.

Connor, Richard A. and Jeffrey P. Davidson. *Marketing Your Consulting and Professional Services*. New York: Wiley, 1990.

Coppett, John I. and William A. Staples. *Professional Selling: A Relationship Management Process*. Cincinnati: South-Western, 1990.

Dalrymple, Douglas J. *Sales Management: Concepts and Cases*, 4th ed. New York: Wiley, 1992.

Davis, Lou Ellen. *Teleprospecting: Warming Up the Cold Call to Increase Sales*. Englewood Cliffs, N.J.: Prentice Hall, 1993.

Fidel, Stanley Leo. *Start-Up Telemarketing: How to Launch a Profitable Sales Operation*. New York: Wiley, 1987.

Freestone, Julie and Janet Brusse. *Telemarketing Basics*. Los Altos, Calif.: Crisp Publications, 1989.

Futrell, Charles M. *ABC's of Selling*, 2d ed. Homewood, Ill.: Irwin, 1988.

Garofalo, Gene. *Sales Manager's Desk Book*. Englewood Cliffs, N.J.: Prentice-Hall, 1988.

Hair, Joseph F., Francis L. Notturno, and Frederick A. Russ. *Effective Selling*, 8th ed. Cincinnati: South-Western, 1991.

Harlan, Raymond C. and Walter B. Woolfson, Jr. *Telemarketing that Works: How to Create a Winning Program for Your Company*. Chicago: Probus, 1991.

Ingram, Thomas N. and Raymond W. LaForge. *Sales Management: Analysis and Decision Making*, 2d ed. Fort Worth, Tex.: Dryden, 1992.

Johnson, H. Webster and Anthony J. Faria. *Creative Selling*, 4th ed. Cincinnati: South-Western, 1987.

Johnston, Karen and Jean Withers. *Selling Strategies for Service Businesses*. Bellingham, Wash.: Self-Counsel Press, 1988.

Kotler, Philip and Paul N. Bloom. *Marketing Professional Services*. Englewood Cliffs, N.J.: Prentice-Hall, 1984.

Lovelock, Christopher H. *Services Marketing*, 2d ed. Englewood Cliffs, N.J.: Prentice-Hall, 1990.

McHatton, Robert J. *Total Telemarketing*. New York: Wiley, 1988.

Maciuba-Koppel, Darlene. *Professional Tactics and Strategies for Instant Results*. New York: Sterling, 1992.

Mahfood, Phillip E. *Teleselling: High Performance Business-to-Business Phone Selling*. Chicago: Probus, 1993.

Masser, Barry Z. *Complete Handbook of All-Purpose Telemarketing Scripts*. Englewood Cliffs, N.J.: Prentice-Hall, 1990.

Pederson, Carlton A. and Milburn D. Wright. *Selling: Principles and Methods*, 9th ed. Homewood, Ill.: Irwin, 1987.

Pesce, Vince. *A Complete Manual of Professional Selling*. New York: Prentice Hall Press, 1989.

Richardson, Linda. *Selling by Phone: How to Reach and Sell Customers in the Nineties*. New York: McGraw-Hill, 1992.

Slutsky, Jeff. *Streetsmart Teleselling: The 33 Secrets*. Englewood Cliffs, N.J.: Prentice-Hall, 1990.

Stone, Bob and John Wyman. *Successful Telemarketing*, 2d ed. Lincolnwood, Ill.: NTC, 1991.

9/   SALES PROMOTION

Sales promotion is a powerful ingredient of the firm's marketing mix. Companies depend on sales promotion to aid and enhance their advertising and personal selling efforts. Manufacturers use it to assist intermediaries in moving consumer and/or industrial goods and services. Wholesalers, retailers, and service firms rely on it to stimulate sales. A complex element, sales promotion embraces a wide array of tools, among them:

Advertising specialties	P.O.P. displays
Anniversary promotions	Premiums
Contests	Preseason sales
Coupons	Price promotions
Credit	Promotional allowances
Demonstrations	Rainchecks
Displays	Rebates
Exhibits	Sampling
Fashion shows	Sweepstakes
Games	Tie-in promotions
Giveaways	Trade-in promotions
PMs (spiffs)	Trading stamps

PROBLEM INDICATORS IN THE SALES PROMOTION AREA

Devote immediate attention to your company's sales promotion activities if you encounter any of the following:

- Disappointment over the results of recent promotions
- Rising expenditures for sales promotion
- Evidence of inadequate promotional planning

- Negligence in tying promotions into media advertising
- Promotions poorly coordinated with other departments
- Unattractive displays—or displays that lack excitement
- Improper handling and/or storage of display equipment, materials, and accessories
- Poor planning by the public relations section
- Dissatisfaction with ongoing public relations programs
- An apparent reluctance to participate in community affairs
- Inability to communicate effectively with one or more of the firm's "publics"
- Too little favorable publicity carried by the media
- Instances of unfavorable publicity

To effect rapid change and improvement in the sales promotion end of your business, launch an immediate investigation of the areas targeted in figure 9-1.

THIS PROMOTION CALENDAR WILL SEND YOUR SALES SKY-HIGH

To maintain a desirable level of sales all throughout the year, determine all promotions long in advance. Set a timetable into place. You'll need time to purchase and prepare the necessary materials, assign display personnel, instruct your salespeople, and tie the promotions into media advertising.

—Tip 159—

For optimum results, work up a six-month promotion schedule well in advance.

To help you in your promotion planning, use the calendar guide in figure 9-2. Initiate your planning by scheduling promotions for:

- The customary time-based events
- Other significant promotional events
- Price-oriented promotions
- Service promotions

Figure 9-1. Aspects of sale promotion to target for investigation

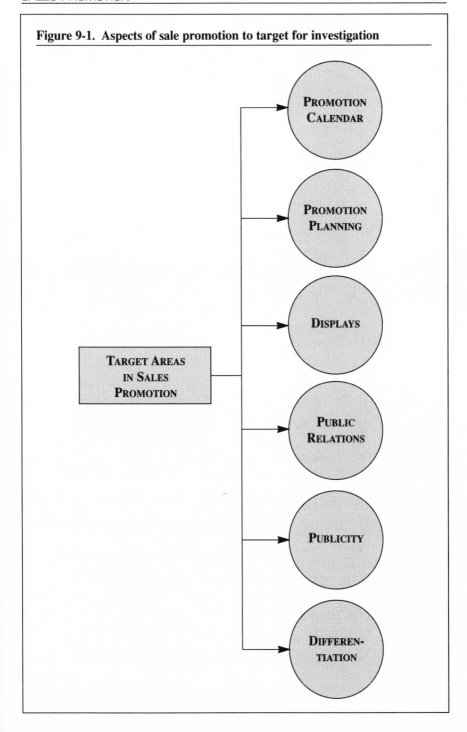

Figure 9-2. Blank promotion calendar for first six months

Week	January	February	March	April	May	June
1						
2						
3						
4						

Enter the information in your promotion calendar, month by month, and under the appropriate weeks.

—Tip 160—

Block out periods for your customary time-based events.

First, select inclusive dates for your firm's anniversary promotion. Then schedule traditional holiday events, such as:

Valentine's Day	Labor Day
Easter	Halloween
Mother's Day	Thanksgiving
Father's Day	Christmas

Retailers may wish to schedule additional promotions for other popular occasions: Presidents' Day, St. Patrick's Day, Pre- and Post-Easter, Back-to-School, Columbus Day, Pre-Thanksgiving, Pre- and Post-Christmas, White Sale, and so on.

—Tip 161—

Identify and schedule other significant promotional events.

Continue filling in unassigned blocks of time with other promotions that you believe will be successful. Consider such suggestions as:

- A contest, game, or sweepstakes
- An exhibit
- A fashion show
- A grand opening (of a new plant or store unit)
- A tie-in promotion
- A trade show

—Tip 162—

Integrate price-oriented promotions into your semiannual calendar.

Some companies offer special sales events rarely, no more than once or twice each year. Other firms offer price promotions every month, and even more often. Unless these sales-stimulating affairs run counter to your company's philosophy, plan one or two of them for each semiannual period. Tie them to such themes as a buyers' sale, manager's sale, anniversary sale, or midnight madness sale.

—Tip 163—

Consider promoting one or two store services.

Look through your calendar for weeks to which no promotion has yet been assigned. Select one or two of your regular services for promotion and enter the information in the proper empty block(s). (See figure 9-3 for a list of the more commonly seen store services.)

UNUSUAL WAYS TO DEVISE MORE PRODUCTIVE PROMOTIONS

As you discuss future promotions, stimulate your thinking by seeking answers to the "five W's:

- WHO will be involved? (Customers, employees, neighborhood people or stores, other businesses, celebrities, and so on)
- WHAT needs to be done?
- WHEN should the promotion take place?
- WHERE should it take place?
- WHY should we run the promotion?

Figure 9-3. Retail services

Alterations	Monogramming
Bulletin boards	Music
Check acceptance	Parking
Consumer information	Quantity discounts
Convenient store hours	Refreshments
Credit	Restrooms
Delivery service	Returns and adjustments
Engraving	Shopping carts
Equipment rental	Telephones
Gift certificates	Water fountains
Gift wrapping	

—Tip 164—

Apply creative thinking techniques to your promotion planning.

In chapter 5, you learned how to use brainstorming and other creative approaches to generate ideas for new products and/or services. The same methods can be applied to producing concepts for exciting new promotions.

—Tip 165—

Evaluate concepts for new promotions with this handy chart.

Once you've come up with a list of new promotion ideas, you'll need some way of evaluating these concepts and choosing the more promising ones. Figure 9-4 displays a sample chart for this purpose. The form contains the following five criteria; their assigned weights appear between parentheses:

- Estimated cost (5X)
- Feasibility (2X)

Figure 9-4. Rating chart for promotion ideas

(Weights)	Estimated Cost (5x)	CRITERIA Feasibility (2x)	Sales Potential (5x)	Effect on Employees (3x)	Effect on Customers (3x)	Score
Idea Summaries: (Short description)						
1.						
2.						
3						
4.						
5.		*****				
10.						

- Sales potential (5X)
- Effect on employees (3X)
- Effect on customers (3X)

Follow this scoring procedure:

- For each idea, total the weighted figures across the page.

- Enter the total, or weighted score, in the last column.

- To obtain the actual score, divide the weighted score by 18. (The column weights were $5 + 2 + 5 + 3 + 3 = 18$.)

- When you've completed the sheet, choose from among the top-rated concepts.

You may wish to add to or substitute others for the criteria indicated in figure 9-4. You'll also need to decide, in light of your priorities, how much weight to assign to each criterion.

SECRETS OF SUPERIOR DISPLAYS

Effective displays attract the attention of prospective buyers, arouse their interest, prompt some people to buy, and generally support efforts at personal selling. They also contribute to the firm's image. To ensure better displays, you'll need to devote time and effort to such aspects of visual merchandising (as the larger retailers call it) as:

- Caring for display equipment, furnishings, and accessories

- Choosing merchandise to put on display

- Building displays according to the basic principles of design

- Allocating display space judiciously

- Using attractive color schemes

- Selecting appropriate themes for your displays

—Tip 166—

Keep display equipment, furnishings, and accessories clean and fresh looking.

Set up a system for cleaning, storing, and otherwise maintaining in excellent condition all display materials and equipment. For however long it's up, each display should look new, fresh, spotlessly clean, and attractive.

See figure 9-5 for the more popular types of display materials and equipment used by retail companies.

Figure 9-5. Display materials and equipment

Fixtures, Furnishings, and Stands:

aisle tables	easels
bins	ladders
bowls	mirrors
chairs	racks
booths	shelves
curtains	stands
dumbbells	tables

Materials:

burlap	foils
carpet	grass mats
cellophanes	papers
fall leaves	ribbons
felt	satins

Signing:

backgrounds	posters
banners	price tickets
pennants	signs

Decorations and props:

baseballs	goblins
baskets	hearts
bats	lights
boats	party hats
bunnies	reindeer
Christmas tree/decorations	Santas
cornucopia	shamrocks
Cupids	skis
dolls	sleds
elves	sleighs
flags	straw hats
firecrackers	streamers
flowers	turkeys
ghosts	witches

Accessory equipment:

ceiling turners	music/sound equipment
color wheels	spotlights
colored lights	turntables
mechanical figures	

—Tip 167—

Select the right merchandise to display.

In your displays, try to feature merchandise that is both timely and popular. Choose goods that have been well-advertised and that are currently in demand. Offer them at selling prices that are equal to or, preferably, below those of your competitors.

—Tip 168—

Follow the basic principles of design when putting up displays.

Effective displays are works of art. Like all artistic creations, they should incorporate these basic principles of design:

- **Unity**. Arrange all elements of a display (fixtures, stands, trays, props, merchandise, colors, signs, and other materials) so that to viewers the display appears as one harmonious unit.

- **Balance**. A display shows formal balance if, when an imaginary line is drawn down the middle of it, viewers perceive both sides as of equal weight or importance. More excitement may be created by setting up informally balanced displays, where one side draws more attention than the other. Both types of balance are accomplished by the right placement and distribution of merchandise, shapes, sizes, colors, stands, and other display components.

- **Proportion**. Each display component should appear in correct proportion to the other elements and to the entire display itself.

- **Contrast**. Occasionally, heighten viewer interest by using contrasting shapes, colors, lighting, merchandise, backgrounds, or other display elements.

- **Dominance**. A display can be strengthened by positioning a single element so that viewer attention is drawn first to that element and then to the balance of the display.

—Tip 169—

For each display, select the pattern that will yield the best results.

Whether intended as part of a window display or to stand alone on a floor or a shelf, each display should follow a set pattern if it is to be effective. Here are the patterns most frequently used by display personnel:

- **Step pattern**. This is the most popular and most versatile arrangement. Position several trays in step formation, one above the next, and each higher tray set back an inch or two from the one below it. Trays may be rectangular, square, circular, or oval in shape.

- **Pyramid pattern**. This is a solid-looking, four-sided geometric arrangement. First, merchandise is laid out to form a wide, flat, square base. A pyramid is then erected on the base by adding more goods gradually and indenting each new level somewhat from the one directly below, until the top, or apex, is reached.

- **Fan pattern**. This arrangement is frequently used to display a large quantity of some featured item. One or two of the articles are centered at the pointed tip of the fan. More are then added, spreading out gradually in fan-like fashion as the height of the display increases. (*Note*: the fan design can also be displayed horizontally, on a single flat plane.)

- **Zigzag pattern**. This design is reminiscent of both the step and the pyramid patterns. Three or more trays on which merchandise is displayed are arranged in step formation. The bottom tray carries the most merchandise. The next higher tray displays fewer goods and may be either set in from or pushed out more than the tray beneath it. On the third tray (counting up from the bottom), even less merchandise appears—and the tray is positioned in an opposite direction to the second tray. And so it goes, until the display unit is complete. To the viewer, then, the display appears to "zig and zag."

—Tip 170—

Build viewer interest and excitement by introducing special effects on occasion.

For more attention-getting value, consider adding such special effects to your displays as:

- Special lighting (flashing or colored lights, color wheels)

- Movement (turntables, ceiling turners, mechanical figures)

- Sound (music, talk, window tappers)

- Sight and sound (color TVs)

—Tip 171—

Keep all displays fresh looking and change them regularly.

Tie planned changes in all displays to your semiannual promotion calendar. In busy areas, retailers generally dress their windows every two or three weeks and redo interior displays at least once a month.

—Tip 172—

Allocate display space judiciously.

Plan carefully when selecting selling space for displays. So much space within a retail store needs to be assigned to work activity, storage, and restrooms that every square foot of selling space becomes crucial to the operation. After all, the selling area is the only area that produces income for the retailer.

Determine the key spots in the store for effective displays: show windows, wall shelves, shadow boxes, and floor areas. Position displays of impulse and other convenience goods at checkouts and in other high-traffic locations. Where you can, build higher displays to increase space productivity.

—Tip 173—

Make effective use of signs.

Signs are necessary and helpful adjuncts to most displays. Although some signs within the retail facility serve to offer directions, designate departments, or announce current or future promotions, most store signs are designed to help sell

goods and services. Whatever their purpose, your signs should look both fresh
and professionally done at all times.

—Tip 174—

Select attractive color schemes for your displays.

Introduce and emphasize color in your displays. Colors catch the eye, setting the mood for and lending excitement to a display. However, they need to be
well coordinated so that they form pleasant and harmonious combinations.

Red, yellow, and blue are known as the primary colors. Combinations of
these hues lead to secondary colors. Green is an example of a secondary color; it's
produced by combining blue and yellow.

Among the more popular color schemes are:

- **Monochromes.** Monochromatic displays show two or more tints or shades of
  the same color—for example, nile green and moss green; sky blue, copen blue,
  and navy blue.

- **Complementary color combinations.** These involve choosing two contrasting colors that are equidistant from one another on the color wheel, such as
  orange and blue or yellow and violet.

- **Triadic color combinations.** These involve three colors that are equidistant
  from one another on the color wheel. Red, blue, and yellow form a triadic color
  scheme.

- **Tone-on-tone displays.** These combine two colors that are close to each other,
  such as yellow and yellow green.

- **Analogous color combinations.** In such schemes, three or more different colors adjacent to each other on the color wheel are used. Red, red-orange, and
  yellow form an analogous color combination.

—Tip 175—

Build displays around appropriate themes.

Creating a display around a specific topic or theme makes for a more compelling display. Most holiday themes are not only effective but are also looked

forward to by potential buyers. Nonholiday themes as well can be woven into great displays.

See figure 9-6 for themes that are popular with retail companies; these are arranged according to the calendar.

—Tip 176—

Define your company's publics.

The typical business organization needs to establish effective two-way communication with the following publics:

- Customers (consumers, dealers)

- Employees

- Stockholders

- Suppliers

- The local community

- The greater community

- Government (at all levels)

—Tip 177—

Plan a strong, year-round public relations program for each of your publics.

TECHNIQUES FOR DEVELOPING BETTER PUBLIC RELATIONS

To the astute businessperson, the term "public relations" represents nothing less than open, honest, and continuous two-way communication between a company and its publics. The primary purpose behind this steady interchange of information is to build and sustain favorable public attitudes over the long term.

Here are just a few of the many activities your company can and should engage in to foster goodwill:

Figure 9-6. Popular display themes

Month	Themes
January	Happy New Year! White Sale Winter Jamboree Martin Luther King's Birthday June in January
February	Lincoln's Birthday Valentine's Day President's Day Washington's Birthday
March/April	St. Patrick's Day Spring Festival Easter Passover
May	Mother's Day Armed Forces Day Graduation (college) Memorial Day
June	Flag Day Father's Day Graduation (high school) Summer Preview
July	Independence Day Vacation Time Fun in the Sun Barbecue Time Midsummer Madness
August	Summer Clearance
September	Back-to-School Labor Day Rosh Hashanah Fall Preview
October	Oktoberfest Columbus Day Harvest Time United Nations Day Halloween

---

Figure 9-6. (continued)

November	Election Day
	Veterans Day
	Fall Clearance
	Thanksgiving
December	Winter Jamboree
	Hanukkah
	Christmas

- Participate in community life (by joining civic and other types of associations as well as the local chamber of commerce; by cooperating with various community organizations; by playing a part in community celebrations and other special events)

- Sponsor a local team, neighborhood beautification program, recycling drive, blood-donor program, or some other worthwhile cause

- Contribute to one or more charities

- Conduct an annual open-house affair

—Tip 178—

Prepare now for next year's anniversary promotion.

Start preparing for next year's anniversary celebration as soon as you've finished evaluating this year's event. Also, develop a powerful grand-opening promotion for each new plant, store, or warehouse you plan to open.

TIPS ON GETTING LOTS OF FREE PUBLICITY

Encourage publicity coverage by giving the media the kinds of stories they look for. In addition to providing the details of anniversary and grand-opening events, offer newsworthy stories about:

- Appearances by celebrities

- Changes in top management

- The introduction of new products, product lines, or services

- Significant promotional events

- Important speeches delivered by company executives

- Stories about employees, for example: membership in local organizations, participation in community events, published articles or books, unusual hobbies, achievements, speeches given, awards received, and so on.

—Tip 179—

Distribute copies of each news release to all local media.

Every publicity release should be well written and look professional. Keep a media reference file in which are listed the names, job titles, addresses, and telephone numbers of the people to whom releases should be sent.

HOW TO DIFFERENTIATE YOUR FIRM FROM THOSE OF YOUR COMPETITORS

Yes, you've been running your business as best you can in this highly competitive economy of ours. Through your dealings with customers, your advertising and promotion, the products and/or services you offer, and your public relations programs, you've already built up your firm's image. More likely than not, you're fairly confident that, to the people or organizations you serve or want to reach, that image is a favorable one.

Why not take a reading on this? You can find out what people think of your operation. Certainly, it should prove useful to learn of your firm's deficiencies, if any, as well as its merits. Once you know about its strengths and weaknesses, you can play up the former and strengthen the latter, reinforcing your position in the economy.

—Tip 180—

Identify your company's strengths and weaknesses.

Through simple research, you can quickly learn how your customers regard your company. You'll need a special tool for this purpose; it's called a "semantic differential instrument." This survey questionnaire contains a set of scales designed to tap the opinions that people may hold about a company or, for that matter, about any object whatsoever. Each scale consists of a pair of opposite words or phrases; these are separated by a number of spaces. (An example of this type of instrument is shown in figure 9-7.)

How to Conduct the Survey

If you sell directly to consumers, ask at least forty of your customers to respond to the survey. Tell them that the information they provide will help you serve them better in the future. Give each person a copy of the form and a pencil. Instruct your customer to read each scale carefully and then place a check mark over the dash in the column that most closely parallels his or her opinion about the particular item.

If you sell to businesses and/or other types of organizations, you'll need to conduct the survey through the mails. Send each customer on your books a survey instrument along with a letter of explanation and clear directions for completing the form. Although the form shown in figure 9-7 is obviously intended for use by retail firms, you can easily adapt it for surveying manufacturing, wholesaling, and service enterprises by substituting other "polar phrases" for those that clearly apply only to retailers.

Here is the procedure for tabulating and scoring the information gathered with the instrument:

1. Count the number of completed survey forms you've managed to collect. Jot down the total at the top of a blank form. (You'll be using this copy as a worksheet for tabulating and scoring the survey data.)

2. Start with the first item (or "scale") on your worksheet:

Warm atmosphere ___ ___ ___ ___ ___ ___ ___ Cold atmosphere

Go through the entire batch, one by one, counting the number of check marks that appear over the first dash in column 1 (under "Extremely"). Enter the total over the corresponding dash on your worksheet.

3. Continue across the first scale, totaling the check marks in each of the six other columns and entering these totals over the appropriate dashes on your worksheet. At this point, the line will look something like this (with different totals, of course):

Warm atmosphere 2 9 34 8 2 1 0 Cold atmosphere

Figure 9-7. An instrument for surveying customers' opinions

	Extremely (1)	Very (2)	Some-what (3)	Can't Decide (4)	Some-what (5)	Very (6)	Extremely (7)	
Warm atmosphere	—	—	—	—	—	—	—	Cold atmosphere
Wide assortment	—	—	—	—	—	—	—	Narrow assortment
Low prices	—	—	—	—	—	—	—	High prices
Good quality merchandise	—	—	—	—	—	—	—	Poor quality merchandise
Convenient store hours	—	—	—	—	—	—	—	Inconvenient store hours
Speedy checkout	—	—	—	—	—	—	—	Slow checkout
Courteous employees	—	—	—	—	—	—	—	Discourteous employees
Attractive displays	—	—	—	—	—	—	—	Unattractive displays
Good service	—	—	—	—	—	—	—	Poor service
Easy to return goods	—	—	—	—	—	—	—	Hard to return goods
Popular styles	—	—	—	—	—	—	—	Unpopular styles
Competent salespeople	—	—	—	—	—	—	—	Incompetent salespeople
Appealing advertising	—	—	—	—	—	—	—	Unappealing advertising
Liberal credit policy	—	—	—	—	—	—	—	Strict credit policy

4. Follow the procedure outlined above in steps 2 through 4 with the remaining scales on the survey instrument. After you complete this step, you'll be ready to weigh and score the survey slips.

5. Look at your worksheet. Proceeding down each column this time (instead of going across the sheet), begin working with column 2 and the second scale. Multiply by 2 each number entered in column 2 for all the remaining scales. Cross out your original tallies and write in the new figures. (Note that we don't need to do this with the counts in the first column since 1 multiplied by itself is still 1!)

6. Continue along in the same fashion, multiplying the entries in column 3 by 3, those in column 4 by 4, and so on—all the way through to the last column (7).

7. Next, add the seven weighted figures across each scale and enter their sum at the end of the line. Now your first scale should resemble the illustration below:

2   18   102   32   10   6   0   170

Warm atmosphere $\underline{2}$ $\underline{9}$ $\underline{34}$ $\underline{8}$ $\underline{2}$ $\underline{1}$ $\underline{0}$ Cold atmosphere

8. *For each scale*, divide the weighted sum at the end of the line by the number of respondents. Cross out the total; replace it with the group's average score; and circle that score. When you've finished the page, you'll have aggregate measures of the group's opinions about the various items listed on the instrument

As an illustration, assume that fifty-six respondents filled out survey forms. Working with the first scale on the page, we divide the weighted total of 170 by 56 and arrive at an average of 3.0 for the group.

Preparing a Profile

Now, you're ready to work up a "profile" of the group's opinions regarding your business enterprise. Take out another blank survey sheet. Look at the average value you obtained for the group on the first item. Place a dot above the dash that is closest to that value. Continue down the list of scales, placing dots where necessary. After you've finished the sheet, use a ruler and pen to draw straight lines from one dot to the next. Once all the dots have been connected, the result will resemble the "profile" in figure 9-8.

As you study the profile, note the following with regard to the survey instrument itself:

■ Entries in the middle (fourth) column indicate a neutral position, one that's neither positive nor negative in character

Figure 9-8. Profiling company strengths and weaknesses

	Extremely (1)	Very (2)	Some-what (3)	Can't Decide (4)	Some-what (5)	Very (6)	Extremely (7)	
Warm atmosphere								Cold atmosphere
Wide assortment								Narrow assortment
Low prices								High prices
Good quality merchandise								Poor quality merchandise
Convenient store hours								Inconvenient store hours
Speedy checkout								Slow checkout
Courteous employees								Discourteous employees
Attractive displays								Unattractive displays
Good service								Poor service
Easy to return goods								Hard to return goods
Popular styles								Unpopular styles
Competent salespeople								Incompetent salespeople
Appealing advertising								Unappealing advertising
Liberal credit policy								Strict credit policy

■ Entries in the first three columns are evidently of a positive nature

■ Entries in columns 5 through 7 reflect negative feelings held by the respondents

Thus, the farther any scale in the profile extends toward the right side of the chart (columns 5, 6, and 7), the greater the urgency for management to take remedial action. In figure 9-8, the group of respondents obviously expressed some degree of dissatisfaction with the firm's assortment, checkout, styles, and credit policy. Moreover, those attributes with ratings of between 3 and 4 also may merit some attention because the group's collective opinions about them ranged from a rather weakly positive "Somewhat" to a "Can't Decide." The attributes were: prices, merchandise quality, service, return policy, and salesperson competency.

Surely, management can take steps to effect improvements in these aspects.

—Tip 181—

**Ascertain your leading competitor's strengths
and weaknesses.**

You can also use the semantic differential instrument to acquire useful insights into your major competitor's operation. Query some of your competitor's customers in the same manner; then follow the identical procedure in tallying their responses and drawing a second profile.

—Tip 182—

Match your firm's profile against that of your competitor.

Enter the scores for your competitor on the same sheet on which you drew your firm's profile. Connect all the nodes with dashes instead of with straight lines, so that you can readily distinguish between the two profiles. At this point, your chart will show two profiles, side by side. (See figure 9-9.)

You can now see where the competitor's strengths and weaknesses lie and compare the differences between the two retailers. As you examine the profiles, note that the first firm (solid lines) rates higher than its competitor on only four scales: atmosphere, assortment, prices, and advertising appeal. It falls behind on all the other scales. More alarming, though, is the wide disparity between the two

Figure 9-9. Comparing profiles: Yours and theirs

	Extremely (1)	Very (2)	Some-what (3)	Can't Decide (4)	Some-what (5)	Very (6)	Extremely (7)	
Warm atmosphere								Cold atmosphere
Wide assortment								Narrow assortment
Low prices								High prices
Good quality merchandise								Poor quality merchandise
Convenient store hours								Inconvenient store hours
Speedy checkout								Slow checkout
Courteous employees								Discourteous employees
Attractive displays								Unattractive displays
Good service								Poor service
Easy to return goods								Hard to return goods
Popular styles								Unpopular styles
Competent salespeople								Incompetent salespeople
Appealing advertising								Unappealing advertising
Liberal credit policy								Strict credit policy

retailers on such attributes as speedy checkout, popular styles, and liberal credit policy.

Armed with such information about your own company and your competition, you can take steps to refine your operation and gradually steer your firm's profile more to the right on the semantic differential chart.

USEFUL REFERENCES

Adelstein, Michael E. and W. Keats Sparrow. *Business Communications*, 2d ed. San Diego, Calif.: Harcourt Brace Jovanovich, 1990.

Baker, Kim and Sunny Baker. *How to Promote, Publicize, and Advertise Your Growing Business*. New York: Wiley, 1992.

Brezin, Tamara and William Robinson. *Sales Promotion Handbook*, 8th ed. Chicago: Dartnell, 1994.

Burstiner, Irving. *Basic Retailing*, 2d ed. Homewood, Ill.: Irwin, 1991.

———. *Mail Order Selling*, 3rd ed. New York: Wiley, 1995.

———. *Start and Run Your Own Profitable Service Business*. Englewood Cliffs, N.J.: Prentice Hall, 1993.

———. *The Small Business Handbook*, rev. ed. New York: Simon & Schuster, 1994.

Connor, Richard A. and Jeffrey P. Davidson. *Marketing Your Consulting and Professional Services*, 2d ed. New York: Wiley, 1990.

Depaola, Helena and Carol S. Mueller. *Marketing Today's Fashion*, 2d ed. Englewood Cliffs, N.J.: Prentice-Hall, 1986.

Edwards, Charles M. and Carl F. Lebowitz. *Retail Advertising and Sales Promotion*, 4th ed. Englewood Cliffs, N.J.: Prentice-Hall, 1981.

Fletcher, Tana and Julia Rockler. *Getting Publicity*. Bellingham, Wash.: Self-Counsel Press, 1990.

Govoni, N. et al. *Promotional Management*. Englewood Cliffs, N.J.: Prentice-Hall, 1986.

Harper, C.R. *Mailing List Strategies: A Guide to Direct Mail Success*. New York: McGraw-Hill, 1986.

Katzenstein, Herbert and William S. Sachs. *Direct Marketing*. Columbus: Merrill, 1986.

Kremer, John. *The Complete Mail Order Sourcebook*. New York: Wiley, 1992.

Mills, Kenneth H. and Judith E. Paul. *Applied Visual Merchandising*, 2d ed. Englewood Cliffs, N.J.: Prentice-Hall, 1988.

Phillips, Pamela M. et al. *Fashion Sales Promotion: The Selling Behind the Selling*. New York: Wiley, 1985.

Putman, Anthony O. *Marketing Your Services: A Step-by-Step Guide for Small Businesses and Professionals*. New York: Wiley, 1989.

Ross, Marilyn and Thomas Ross. *Big Marketing Ideas for Small Service Businesses.* Homewood, Ill.: Dow Jones-Irwin, 1990.

Shimp, Terence A. and M. Wayne Delozier. *Promotion Management and Marketing Communications.* New York: Dryden, 1986.

Slutsky, Jeff. *Streetsmart Marketing.* New York: Wiley, 1989.

Smith, Jeanette. *The Publicity Kit.* New York: Wiley, 1991.

Spitzer, Harry and F. Richard Schwartz. *Inside Retail Sales Promotion and Advertising.* New York: Harper & Row, 1982.

Stanley, Richard E. *Promotion: Advertising, Publicity, Personal Selling, Sales Promotion,* 2d ed. Englewood Cliffs, N.J.: Prentice-Hall, 1982.

Wilson, Jerry R. *Word-of-Mouth Marketing.* New York: Wiley, 1994.

10/ REVAMP YOUR DISTRIBUTION METHODS

Distribution brings in sales revenues. Distribution planning involves making policy decisions and devising tactical measures for moving company goods and services from the manufacturer or producer to consumers or organizational buyers. Distribution management seeks to strike a balance between quality customer service and distribution costs.

In this area of operations, you need to examine:

- The distribution policies you've adopted

- Your distribution approaches—how you've planned to get your goods into the hands of consumers or organizational users

- Channel arrangements now in place

- Level of cooperation among channel members

- Management of the warehousing and physical distribution functions

- Plans for future growth

PROBLEM INDICATORS IN THE DISTRIBUTION AREA

Be on the lookout for these signs of upcoming problems in the distribution end of your business:

- Dissatisfaction with the extent of your distribution

- Inability to interest quantity buyers in carrying your products

- Communication difficulties along the marketing channels

- Channel conflicts; for example: one or more channel participants encroaching on other members' territories

- Distributors clamoring for cooperative advertising monies and/or advertising aids

- Customers demanding higher discounts, extended dating, or better terms

- Customers delaying payment of bills

- Too many returns

- An inordinate number of customer complaints

- Lack of coordination among departments

- Routing errors

- Mounting transportation costs

- Delivery errors (wrong merchandise and/or quantities, delivery delays, too many back orders, and so on)

- Inconsistent customer service

- Difficulty in locating stored goods

- Inefficient warehouse layout

- Lack of proper warehousing equipment

- Discrepancies between book and actual inventories

Those aspects of distribution worthy of your investigation and fine-tuning are presented in figure 10-1.

SUGGESTIONS FOR IMPROVING YOUR DISTRIBUTION APPROACHES

Begin your investigation into the distribution function by reconsidering two policy decisions you may have made. The first involves the extent of distribution you preferred for your company; the second deals with the method you chose for delivering your products and/or services to their intended users.

—Tip 183—

Review your current distribution policies.

With respect to the extent of distribution desired, review the following three possibilities:

Figure 10-1. Distribution aspects to target for investigation

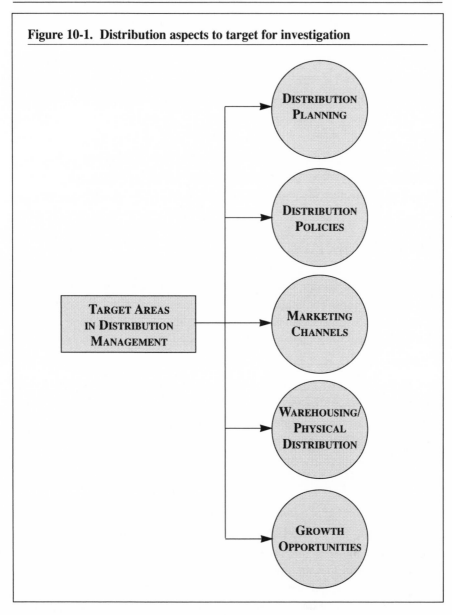

1. **Exclusive Distribution.** Contracting to sell the company's products to only one wholesaler or large retailer in each geographic area. (Usually, management chooses this approach in order to project a high-quality image, maintain control over the channels of distribution, and earn substantial gross profit on the goods that are sold.)

2. **Selective Distribution.** Offering the company's products and/or services for sale to a limited number of wholesalers who field sizable and well-experienced salesforces, are financially healthy, and are prepared to give special attention to the company's product/service line.

3. **Intensive Distribution.** Opening up the entire region, country, or world by selling company products to any and all distributors who are willing to purchase and resell them.

Reexamine your position. Moving down from choice 1 to choice 2 will add substantially to your sales volume; electing choice 3 will multiply your sales even more. Can you handle such volume?

Distribution Channels

In marketing, manufacturers and producers arrange for their products and/or services to be forwarded to final users, whether they are individual consumers or organizations. Some companies sell directly to their customers, as per this diagram below for a direct channel:

Manufacturer ——————————————————→ User

However, the vast majority of companies go through more complex channels, contracting with intermediary institutions to help move the goods and/or services along to their final destinations. Such arrangements may involve one, two, or three distinct types of intermediaries, as indicated below:

Manufacturer ——————————→ Retailer ——————————→ User

Manufacturer————→ Wholesaler ————→ Retailer ————→ User

Manufacturer——→ Agent ——→ Wholesaler——→ Retailer ——→ User

The shorter the channel, that is to say, the fewer the number of intermediaries involved, the faster the products and/or services will move and the greater will be the control that the manufacturer or producer can exert over the goods. Perishables and semiperishable goods, items of high unit value, and technical products usually travel through shorter channels; longer channels are typical for popular products of low-to-moderate unit value.

Wholesalers: Retail firms and wholesaling establishments are welcome participants in the distribution channels. Wholesalers, also referred to as distributors or "jobbers," buy goods in large quantities from manufacturers or producers and then resell the goods in smaller amounts to retailers, industrial customers, institutions, government agencies, and other kinds of organizations.

Brief descriptions of various types of wholesaling intermediaries, including brokers and agents, are offered in figure 10-2.

—Tip 184—

Smooth out the difficulties and promote cooperation among channel members.

Whenever two or more firms cooperate distributing goods and/or services, occasional conflicts may be expected to develop. A manufacturing company may complain that its channel intermediaries:

- Promote other brands or their own house brand instead of the manufacturer's brand

- Only purchase some, not all, of their products or services

- Pay their bills late

- Request changes in packaging

- Ask for more extended terms and larger cash discounts

- Want faster and more frequent deliveries

- Complain about product quality

- Demand more promotional support

On the other hand, wholesalers and retailers may complain that the manufacturer:

- Offers one or more products of inferior quality

- Prices its goods and/or services too high

- Ought to provide more cooperative advertising money

- Has an unfair return policy

- Needs to strengthen its warranties

- Should preprice the goods

The best approach to minimizing channel conflict is to work hard at improving communication between or among the participants.

—Tip 185—

Explore alternatives and make decisions.

Figure 10-2. Channel intermediaries: Wholesalers, brokers, and agents

Merchant wholesaler. Most prevalent among wholesale establishments, this intermediary provides goods and/or services to retail companies for resale to consumers.

Industrial distributor. This industrial counterpart to the merchant wholesaler supplies businesses, institutions, government agencies, and other types of organizations with goods and services they need for internal use.

Full-service wholesaler. A company that performs all of the activities expected of a wholesaler in forwarding goods through channels of distribution: buying quantities of goods, maintaining inventory, selling, extending credit, arranging for shipment, supplying information, and so on.

There are three types of full-service operations.

1. The *general merchandise wholesaler* carries a number of merchandise lines.
2. The *single-line wholesaler* offers a complete assortment of goods within one major line of trade.
3. The *specialty wholesaler* supplies a narrow range of products within a single merchandise line.

Limited-service wholesaler. A firm that provides some, but not all, of the traditional wholesaling functions; for example: doesn't extend credit or doesn't keep inventory on hand.

The limited-service (or limited-function) wholesalers are:

1. The *cash-and-carry wholesaler* maintains ample inventory to service area merchants. Retailers stop in to purchase, at wholesale prices, goods that they need in the operation of their business. No credit is offered; instead, the merchants are required to pay on purchase and then take the goods out with them to their vehicles.
2. The *drop shipper*, or *desk jobber*, works with bulky products such as gravel, lumber, and coal. This wholesaler takes orders, sends the orders over to the manufacturer or producer, and requests that the goods be shipped directly to the buyer. The drop shipper pays the supplier for the goods and bills the customer at a price that includes the desired margin of profit.
3. The *mail-order wholesaler* mails catalogs and other advertising literature to prospective buyers. Incoming orders are filled and then shipped via the U.S. Postal Service, United Parcel Service, or some other delivery service.
4. The *rack jobber* places floor stands and other racks in stores at no charge, stocks them with consignment goods, and thereafter visits these locations regularly to freshen up and restock the displays. The retailers pay only for merchandise that has been sold.
5. The *truck jobber* covers a regular route, delivering impulse goods and snack items by truck to food stores. The merchandise is sold on a cash-on-delivery basis.

The **broker** is instrumental in bringing buyers and sellers together and is compensated for his or her efforts by a commission paid by whichever side employs this intermediary.

Figure 10-2. Continued

The **agent** markets goods on behalf of manufacturers or producers. Agent intermediaries who operate in the channels of distribution include:

1. The *selling agent* contracts to accept responsibility for selling a manufacturer's entire output. Generally, this intermediary offers worthwhile advice regarding the product, packaging, pricing, advertising, sales promotion, and other aspects.
2. The *manufacturer's agent*, or *manufacturer's rep(resentative)*, contracts to sell some of a company's production, usually within an assigned territory. Compensation is in the form of a commission on sales brought in. Frequently, this intermediary will carry along one or more additional, noncompeting lines of merchandise.
3. The *commission agent*, or *commission merchant*, typically represents farmers, growers, or ranchers in the sale of agricultural products and livestock. This agent takes in the goods or animals, sells them, deducts a commission for the sale, and forwards the balance of the money to the owner.

If you're in any way dissatisfied with present channel arrangements, prepare to improve your situation. Look to replace any and all unsatisfactory distributors with others who not only are available and of good reputation but also:

■ Command adequate financial resources

■ Manage competent salesforces

■ Are anxious to cooperate

For more control over your products and/or services as well as over the channels of distribution, consider the following possibilities:

■ If you're a manufacturer, weigh the pros and cons of—(a) selling via direct mail, mail order advertising, and catalogs to both retail and wholesale distributors, (b) contracting with a top-rated selling agent to sell off your entire production, (c) establishing a salesforce of your own, and (d) forming a vertical marketing system of the corporate type.

■ If you're a large wholesaler, look into the advantages and drawbacks of creating a wholesaler-sponsored voluntary chain of retailers.

■ If you're a retailer, think about encouraging the formation of a retailer cooperative.

Push and Pull Strategies

The manufacturing company needs to choose whether to adopt a push or a pull strategy for promoting its products. If a push strategy is selected, the manufacturer will advertise directly to its wholesalers and/or retailers to get them to stock up, thereby "pushing" the goods through the distribution channels. Under a pull strategy, the firm will seek to enhance demand by advertising directly to consumers or industrial users; in turn, these people will go to retail stores (their usual sources) to buy, thus "pulling" the goods through the channels.

—Tip 186—

Effect improvements in the warehousing and physical distribution areas.

It's the warehouse manager's job to maintain close control over the company's inventory: to accept incoming goods, keep them safely stored, ensure that quantities are sufficient to meet demand, and ready them for shipment when needed. Holding down warehousing costs is an ancillary, though important, responsibility. Similarly, the traffic manager needs to focus on monitoring and holding down transportation costs when arranging shipments of goods via reliable carriers.

(*Note:* For helpful suggestions in these two areas, see the section in chapter 4 entitled "Ideas for Cutting Warehousing and Delivery Expenses"—especially the "Actions to Consider" listed below tips 83 and 84.)

EXPLORE GROWTH OPPORTUNITIES AND THE FRANCHISE SECTOR

After you've finished auditing and fine-tuning all the major parts of your business machine, you're bound to realize that the effort was indeed worthwhile. Your ascending sales curve should keep on rising; a comparison of your two most recent income statements and balance sheets should reveal impressive gains. At this point, it's time to start thinking about your company's future.

—Tip 187—

Consider your options for expansion.

There are several routes to choose from:

■ **Acquisition.** Buying an established business of the same type as yours. (Not only will this move enable you to apply your experience, skills, and knowledge to an additional enterprise but it may also bring you impressive economies of scale.)

■ **Diversification.** Buying one or more businesses of type(s) unrelated to yours. (The major benefit behind a move of this kind is that it enables you to spread your risk.)

■ **Merger.** Combining with another organization of the same type (a horizontal merger) or solidifying your control over distribution through forward or backward integration (a vertical merger). (Among the rewards a merger may bring are greater financial resources, additional machinery, new products, new customers, and specialized personnel.)

■ **Franchising.** Granting licenses to other people to operate clones of your present business. (A move of this nature will enable you to expand your successful operation quickly by using other people's money.)

—Tip 188—

Weigh the pros and cons of franchising your successful business operation.

A form of licensing, franchising offers people the opportunity to own their own businesses even if they've had no prior business experience. For you, franchising can be your passageway to rapid expansion without risking a heavy investment. Moreover, you'll retain control over this channel of distribution even as you franchise branches of your business all across the country.

Franchisors are already well represented in such fields as the lodging industry, car/truck rental, health and dental services, restaurants, recreational facilities, and business services. Franchising activity is especially heavy in the retail sector, accounting each year for more than one-third of the nation's total retail sales.

Pointers on Franchising

Going the franchise route calls for a distinct and unusual type of operation, much different from the successful business you've been running and want to expand.

It's not an easy road to travel but, if you handle things correctly, this avenue can prove quite lucrative.

Among the many activities you'll need to get involved in are:

■ Structuring an attractive franchise sales program

■ Setting reasonable, and realizable, objectives

■ Preparing a comprehensive prospectus (disclosure statement) that contains all information pertinent to the franchise offer—how much in equity the prospective franchisee will need, the amount of the initial franchise fee, continuing payments to be made, applicable restrictions, territorial protection (if available), sample contract, financial statements of the franchisor, and so on.

■ Hiring an experienced franchise sales manager and setting up a sales organization

■ Developing a program for locating and evaluating prospective franchisees.

■ Searching for suitable locations

■ Designing and building business premises

■ Standardizing products, services, equipment, systems, and procedures

■ Preparing operating manuals and offering operations and management training

■ Providing merchandising counsel

■ Maintaining quality control

■ Giving promotional support

USEFUL REFERENCES

Hunt, Michael and Thomas Speh. *Industrial Marketing Management*, 2d ed. New York: Dryden Press, 1985.

Justis, Robert T. and Richard J. Judd. *Franchising*. Cincinnati: South-Western, 1989.

Levy, Michael and Barton A. Weitz. *Retailing Management*. Homewood, Ill.: Irwin, 1992.

Lewis, Mack O. *How to Franchise Your Business*, 3rd ed. New York: Pilot Books, 1990.

Lowry, James R. et al. *Business in Today's World*. Cincinnati, Ohio: South-Western, 1990.

Rust, Herbert. *Owning Your Own Franchise*. Englewood Cliffs, N.J.: Prentice-Hall, 1991.

Stern, Louis W. and Adel I. El-Ansary. *Marketing Channels*, 4th ed. Englewood Cliffs, N.J.: Prentice-Hall, 1991.

West, Alan. *Manufacturing Distribution and Change: The Total Distribution Concept*. New York: Wiley, 1989.

INDEX